بسم الله الرحمن الرحيم

ABOUT THE AUTHOR

Under the pen-name HARUN YAHYA, the author has published many books on political and faith-related issues. An important body of his work deals with the materialistic world view and the impact of it in world history and politics. (The pen-name is formed from the names 'Harun' [Aaron] and 'Yahya' [John] in the esteemed memory of the two Prophets who struggled against infidelity.)

His works include The 'Secret Hand' in Bosnia, The Holocaust Hoax, Behind the Scenes of Terrorism, Israel's Kurdish Card, A National Strategy for Turkey, Solution: The Morals of the Qur'an, Darwin's Antagonism Against the Turks, The Evolution Deceit, Perished Nations, The Golden Age, The Art of Colour by Allah, The Truth of the Life of This World, Confessions of Evolutionists, The Blunders of Evolutionists, The Qur'an Leads the Way to Science, The Real Origin of Life, Miracles of the Qur'an, The Design in Nature, Self-Sacrifice and Intelligent Behaviour Models in Animals, Eternity Has Already Begun, Children Darwin Was Lying!, The End of Darwinism, The Creation of the Universe, Never Plead Ignorance, Timelessness and the Reality of Fate, The Miracle of the Atom, The Miracle in the Cell, The Miracle of the Immune System, The Miracle in the Eye, The Creation Miracle in Plants, The Miracle in the Spider, The Miracle in the Ant, The Miracle in the Gnat, The Miracle in the Honeybee.

Among his booklets are The Mystery of the Atom, The Collapse of the Theory of Evolution: The Fact of Creation, The Collapse of Materialism, The End of Materialism, The Blunders of Evolutionists 1, The Blunders of Evolutionists 2, The Microbiological Collapse of Evolution, The Fact of Creation, The Collapse of the Theory of Evolution in 20 Questions, The Biggest Deception in the History of Biology: Darwinism.

The author's other works on Quranic topics include: Ever Thought About the Truth?, Devoted to Allah, Abandoning the Society of Ignorance, Paradise, The Theory of Evolution, The Moral Values of the Qur'an, Knowledge of the Qur'an, Qur'an Index, Emigrating for the Cause of Allah, The Character of Hypocrites in the Qur'an, The Secrets of the Hypocrite, The Names of Allah, Communicating the Message and Disputing in the Qur'an, The Basic Concepts in the Qur'an, Answers from the Qur'an, Death Resurrection Hell, The Struggle of the Messengers, The Avowed Enemy of Man: Satan, Idolatry, The Religion of the Ignorant, The Arrogance of Satan, Prayer in the Qur'an, The Importance of Conscience in the Qur'an, The Day of Resurrection, Never Forget, Disregarded Judgements of the Qur'an, Human Characters in the Society of Ignorance, The Importance of Patience in the Qur'an, General Information from the Qur'an, Quick Grasp of Faith 1-2-3, The Crude Reasoning of Disbelief, The Mature Faith, Before You Regret, Our Messengers Say, The Mercy of Believers, The Fear of Allah, The Nightmare of Disbelief, Prophet Isa Will Come, Beauties Presented by the Qur'an for Life, The Iniquity Called "Mockery", The Secret of the Test, The True Wisdom According to the Qur'an, The Struggle with the Religion of Irreligion, Bouquet of the Beauties of Allah 1-2-3-4.

THE
MIRACLE
IN THE
ANT

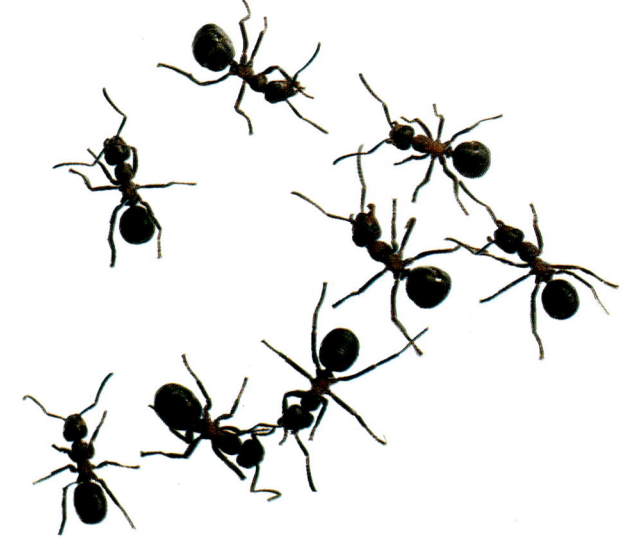

Copyright © Harun Yahya 2000 CE
First Published by Vural Yayıncılık, İstanbul, Turkey in September 1999

First English Edition published in May 2000

Published by:
Ta-Ha Publishers Ltd.
1 Wynne Road
London SW9 OBB
United Kingdom

Website: http://www.taha.co.uk
E-Mail: sales @ taha.co.uk

All rights reserved. No part of this publication may be reproduced, stored in any retrivial system or transmitted in any form or by any methods, electronic, mechanical, photocopying, recording, or otherwise without the prior permission of the publishers.

By Harun Yahya
Translated By: Mustapha Ahmad
Edited By: Abdassamad Clarke

A catalog record of this book is available from the British Library
ISBN 1-84200-016-0

Printed and bound by:
Secil Ofset in İstanbul
Address: Yüzyıl Mahallesi MAS-SIT Matbaacılar Sitesi
4. Cadde No:77 Bağcılar- İstanbul / TURKEY

Website: http: // www.harunyahya.org
http: // www.harunyahya.com
http: // www.harunyahya.net

Ta-Ha Publishers Ltd.
1 Wynne Road London SW9 OBB

THE
MIRACLE
IN THE
ANT

HARUN YAHYA

TO THE READER

The reason why a special chapter is assigned to the collapse of the theory of evolution is that this theory constitutes the basis of all anti-spiritual philosophies. Since Darwinism rejects the fact of creation, and therefore the existence of Allah, during the last 140 years it has caused many people to abandon their faith or fall into doubt. Therefore, showing that this theory is a deception is a very important duty, which is strongly related to the deen. It is imperative that this important service is rendered to all people. Some of our readers may find the chance to read only one of our books. Therefore, we think it appropriate to spare a chapter for a summary of this subject.

Another point to be stressed is related to the content of the book. In all the books of the author, faith-related issues are told in the light of the Qur'anic verses and people are invited to learn Allah's verses and live by them. All the subjects that concern Allah's verses are explained in such a way as to leave no room for doubt or question marks in the reader's mind.

The sincere, plain and fluent style employed ensures that everyone of every age and from every social group can easily understand the books. This effective and lucid way of recounting makes the books read quickly. Even those people who rigorously reject spirituality are influenced by the facts recounted in these books and cannot refute the truthfulness of their contents.

This book and all the other works of the author can be read by individuals or studied in a group at a time of conversation. The reading of the books by a group of readers willing to profit from them will be useful in the sense that readers can relate their own reflections and experiences to one another.

In addition, it will be a great service to the deen to contribute to the presentation and reading of these books, which are written solely for the good pleasure of Allah. All the books of the author are extremely convincing. For this reason, for those who want to communicate the deen to other people, one of the most effective methods is to encourage them to read these books.

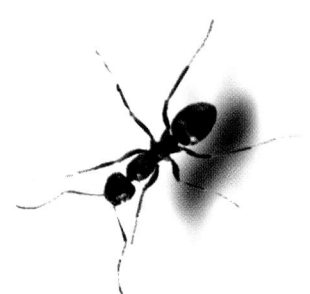

CONTENTS

Preface 9

Introduction 11

Social Life 16

Communication in Society 30

Ant Species 44

Symbiosis 74

Defence and War Tactic 104

Feeding and Hunting 124

Conclusion 132

Evolution Deceit 134

PREFACE

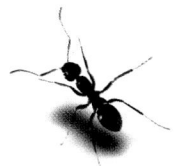

In this book we are going to tell you about a creature that you know quite well, that you meet everywhere without actually giving it much attention, that is highly skillful, highly social and highly intelligent - "The Ant". Our aim is to review the lives full of miracles of these minute creatures that are never of any significance in our daily lives.

Technology, collective work, military strategy, advanced communications network, an astute and rational hierarchy, discipline, perfect city planning... These are fields where human beings may not always be successful enough, but where the ants always are. When you look at these creatures, which are fully armed to defeat tough rivals and to endure the difficult conditions of nature, you may think that all of them are identical. However, each species of the ant genus – and there are thousands of them – has, in fact, different characteristics. We believe that these creatures that have the highest population in the world may open up new horizons for us within the framework of the characteristics referred to above. This book will reveal to us the special and marvelous world of ants. We shall witness the things these ant communities succeed with their tiny bodies and witness that there is absolutely no difference between their fossils, the oldest of which is about 80 million years old, and their counterparts living today, that run to approximately 8800 species.

As we explore the special world of ants, this perfect system will earn our admiration and increase the need for thinking and investigating. At the same time, we shall see the mistakes in the theory of evolution and witness Allah's immaculate creation, which is a tremendously important work. In the Qur'an, the type of person who thinks about nature and thus recognizes the omnipotence of Allah is praised as a model for those who believe. The verses below explain this point fully:

> **In the creation of the heavens and the earth, and the alternation of night and day, there are indeed signs for men of understanding: men who celebrate the praises of Allah, standing, sitting, and lying down on their sides, and contemplate the wonders of creation in the heavens and the earth, (saying): "Our Lord! You have not created all this in vain! Glory be to You! Give us salvation from the penalty of the Fire." (Surat Al 'Imran:190-191)**

We hope that this book causes its readers to think more deeply on and to feel admiration for the superior power and unequaled art of creation of Allah, Who has made all things.

INTRODUCTION

The living beings that have the densest population in the world are the ants. For every seven hundred million ants that come into this world there are only 40 new-born human beings. There is a lot of other amazing information to learn about these creatures.

The ants, one of the most "social" groups among the insect genus, live as societies called "colonies", which are extremely well "organized." Their organization is of such an advanced order that it may be said that in this respect they have a civilization similar to that of humans.

The ants care for their babies, protect their colonies and fight as they produce and store their food. There are even colonies that do "tailoring", that deal in "agriculture" or "animal husbandry". These animals, with their very strong communication network, are so superior as not to be compared to any other organism, with respect to social organization and specialization.

In our day, researchers with superior intelligence and education are working day and night in think tanks formed to formulate successful social organizations and to find lasting solutions to social and economic problems. Ideologues have been producing social models for centuries. Yet when we look at the world in general, no ideal socio-economic social order has so far been reached, in spite of all these intensive efforts. Since the concept of order in human societies has always been based on competition and individual interests, a perfect social order has never been possible. The ants on the other hand, have perpetuated the social system that is ideal for them for millions of years right down to the present day.

Then how can these minute creatures form such an order? This is a question for which an answer must certainly be sought.

Evolutionists, when trying to answer this question, claim that ants evolved 80 million years ago from "Tiphiidae", which is an archaic genus of wasps, and that they started socializing 40 million years ago – suddenly, "at their own discretion" - and that they constitute the highest level of the evolution of insects. However, they do not in any way explain the causes and the process of development of this socialization. The basic mechanism of evolution requires living beings to fight with each other to the end, for their survival. Therefore, each genus and every individual within that genus can think of only itself and its own offspring (Why and how it started thinking of its offspring is another dead end for Evolution, but we are skipping this point for now). It is, of course, unanswered how this type of a "law of evolution" can form a social system with sacrifice right at its core.

The questions to be answered are not limited to these. Could these creatures whose nerve cells for one million of them only weigh 20 grams, have adopted the resolution to socialize in groups "just like that"? Or could they have got together to set the rules for this socializing after adopting such a resolution? Even if we accept that they could, would all of them obey this new system without exception? Have they formed an advanced social order by founding colonies with millions of members after overcoming all these seeming impossibilities?

Then how did a "caste system" emerge out of this struggle? First, this question has to be answered: How has the difference between the queen and the worker developed? Evolutionists at this point will say that a group among the workers abandoned working and developed a physiology different from the worker ants by going through genetic variations over a long period of time. However, we are then faced with the question of how the said "would be queens" were nourished throughout this transformation period. The queen ants do not look for food. They are fed with food brought by the workers. Some workers may have seen themselves as "queens", so how and why have other workers accepted this hierarchy? Furthermore, why have they consented to feed this queen? The "struggle for life" that they are in, according to "evolution", requires that they only think of themselves.

All insects spend most of their time in looking for food. They find

Ant fossil dating back 80 million years. This fossil clearly shows us that ants have not at all changed over 80 millions years.

and they eat food, then they get hungry again and go off to find more food. They also run from danger. When we accept evolution, we also have to accept that the ants too lived "individually" once upon a time, but that one day, millions of years ago, they decided to become socialized. The question then arises as to how they "decided" "to form" this social order without any common communication between themselves, because, according to evolution, communication is a consequence of socializing. Furthermore, the question of how they have developed the genetic mutation required for this socialization has no scientific explanation whatsoever.

In the heavens and the earth there are certainly signs for believers. And in your creation, and in all the creatures that He has spread about, there are signs for people whose faith is sure. (Surat al-Jathiyah: 3-4)

All these arguments take us to a single point: To claim that the ants started "socializing" one day millions of years ago is to break all the basic rules of logic. The only possible explanation is as follows: The social order, of which we shall see the details in the following chapters, was created along with the ants; and this system has not varied since the first ant colony on earth, until today.

When mentioning the bees who have a social order similar to that of the ants, Allah states in the Qur'an that this social order has been "revealed" to them:

> **And your Lord revealed to the bee: "Build dwellings in the mountains and the trees and also in the structures which men erect. Then eat from every kind of fruit and travel the paths of your Lord, which have been made easy for you to follow." From inside them comes a drink of varying colours, containing healing for mankind. There is certainly a sign in that for people who reflect. (Surat an-Nahl: 68-69)**

The verse conveys the message that everything the honey bees do is governed by a "revelation" Allah has given to them. Accordingly, all the "homes", that is, hives - and therefore the entire social order in these hives - and all the work they perform to make honey, are made possible by an inspiration Allah has given them.

When we look at ants, we see that things are no different for them either. Allah has inspired in them a social order also and they abide by it absolutely. This is the reason why each group of ant performs the duty assigned to it perfectly with absolute self-surrender and does not strive for more.

And this is the law of nature. There is no random and coincidental "fight for survival" in nature as purported by evolution and there has never been one. On the contrary, all living creatures eat the "food" specified for them and perform duties Allah assigned to them. Because "there is no living being He (Allah) does not hold by the forelock and inspect." (Surah Hud: 56) and "He (Allah) is the one who gives food." (Surat adh-Dhariyat: 58)

SOCIAL LIFE

We mentioned that ants live in colonies and that a perfect division of labour exists amongst them. When we take a closer look at their systems, we shall also see that they have a pretty interesting social structure. It will also come to our attention that they are capable of sacrifice at a much higher level than humans are. One of the most interesting points is that – compared to humans – they do not know the concepts such as the rich-poor discrimination and the fight for power that are observed in our societies.

Many scientists, who for years have been doing extensive research on ants, have not been able to clarify the subject of their advanced social behaviour. Caryle P. Haskins, Ph.D., the president of the Carnegie Institute at Washington has this to say:

> After 60 years of observation and study, I still marvel at how sophisticated the ants' social behavior is. ...The ants thus make a beautiful model for our use in studying the roots of animal behavior.[1]

Some colonies of ants are so extensive with respect to population and living area, that it is impossible to explain how they can form a perfect order over such a vast area. Therefore, it is not easy not to concur with Dr. Haskins.

As an example of these large colonies we can give the species of ant, called Formica Yesensis, that lives on the Ishikari coast of Africa. This ant colony lives in 45,000 nests connected to each other over an area of 2.7 square kilometres. The colony, which has approximately 1,080,000 queens and 306,000,000 workers has been named the "Super colony" by the researchers. It has been discovered that all production tools and food are exchanged in an orderly fashion within the colony[2]. It is very hard to explain how the ants have maintained this order without any problems, considering the vast area they are living in. We must not forget that various security forces are needed for enforcing law and maintaining social order, even in a civilized country with a low population density. And there is an administrative staff leading and managing these units. Sometimes, it does not become possible to maintain the required order without problems despite all these intense efforts.

Yet in ant colonies there is no need felt for police, gendarmerie or guards. If we consider that actually the duty of the queens, whom we think of as the leaders of the colonies, is just to maintain the species, they do not have a leader or a governor. There is thus no hierarchy based on a chain of command amongst them. Then who is it that lays down this order and maintains its continuity?

In the later chapters of the book we shall find answers to this question and similar others in combination.

The most important feature of ant colonies is their having a full "social life" and their doing everything as a matter of solidarity. In this picture, we see a group of ants that are trying to carry a fruit home together.

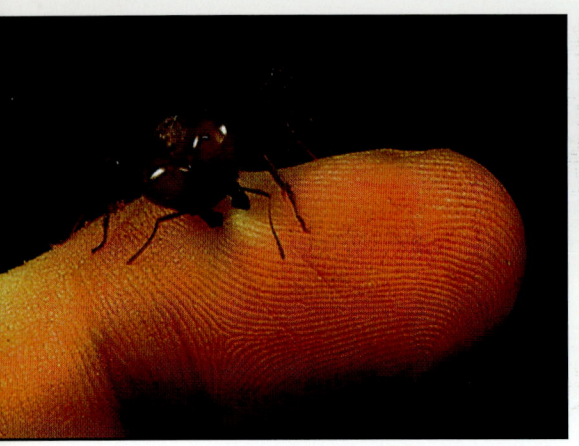

Ants, which are very small creatures, pursue their lives with perfect orderliness in spite of their size.

CASTE SYSTEM

Each ant colony without exception complies strictly with the caste system. This caste system consists of three major parts within a colony.

Members of the first caste are the queen and the males who make reproduction possible. More than one queen may exist in a colony. The queen has assumed the task of reproducing and thus increasing the number of individuals making up the colony. Her body is larger than that of the other ants. The duty of the males on the other hand is just to fertilize the queen. In fact, nearly all of these die after the nuptial flight.

The members of the second caste are the soldiers. These take on duties like the setting up of the colony, finding a new living environment and hunting.

The third caste consists of worker ants. All of the workers are sterile females. They take care of the mother ant and her babies; they clean and feed them. In addition to all these, other jobs in the colony are also under the responsibility of the workers. They build new corridors and new galleries for their nests; they search for food and continually clean up the nest.

The worker and soldier ants also have sub-groups. These are named slaves, thieves, nannies, construction workers and collectors. Each group has a different task. While one group focuses completely on fighting the enemy or hunting, another group builds nests, and yet another one looks after maintenance.

Every individual in the ant colonies does his full share of the work.

None of them worry about the position it is in nor the nature of the job it performs, but it plainly does what is required of it. What is important is the continuity of the colony.

When we think about how this system could have developed, we cannot avoid reaching the fact of creation.

Let us explain why: Where there is perfect order, logically we reach the conclusion that this has certainly been established by a planning mind. For instance, there is a disciplined order in the military; it is obvious that the officers in control of the army have established this order. It would certainly be an absurd idea to assume that all individuals in the army came together on their own and organized themselves and that later on they were grouped in different ranks and started acting in compliance with these ranks. Furthermore, the officers who have established this order have to keep on carrying out inspections of this order so that it may persist without any problems. Otherwise, an army left solely to the troops would soon be transformed into an unruly crowd, regardless of how well disciplined it might have been at the beginning.

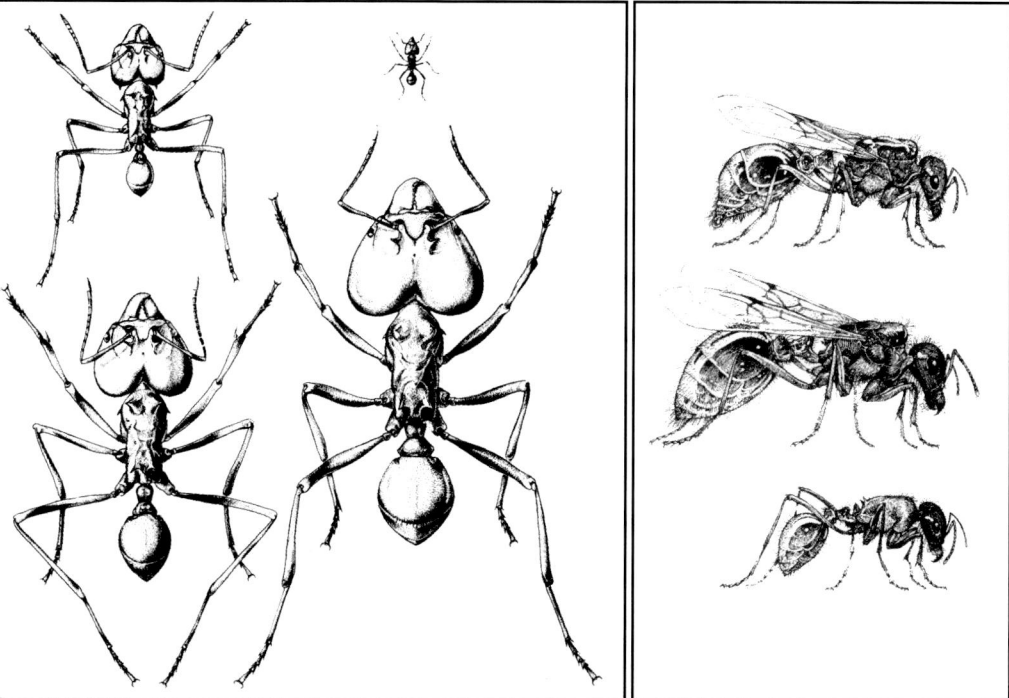

Ants within the same colony who belong to different castes have different physical appearances as well. Each has a physical build appropriate for its job.

The ants also have a discipline very similar to that of the military. Yet the critical aspect is that there is no "officer", that is any organizing administrator, in sight. The various caste systems within the ant colony carry out their duties in a faultless manner; although, yet there is no obvious "central power" which supervises them.

Then the only explanation is that the central will in question is an "invisible" one. The inspiration which is mentioned in the Qur'an with the statement "And your Lord revealed to the bee" (Surat Nahl: 68), is this invisible power.

This will has achieved such tremendous planning that people are in awe of it when they try to analyze it. Such awe and wonderment have been expressed from time to time in various forms by the researchers as well. Evolutionists, who claim that such a perfect system has developed as a result of coincidences, are not able to explain this sacrificial behaviour which is at the core of this system. An article written on this subject in the Journal of *Bilim ve Teknik* indicates this incapability once more:

> The problem is why living beings help each other. According to Darwin's Theory, each living creature fights for his own survival and reproduces. Since helping others would relatively decrease the probability of survival of that living being, this behaviour had to be eliminated by evolution in the long run. Yet it has been observed that living beings may be ready to sacrifice.
>
> A classical form of explaining the fact of sacrifice is that the colonies which are made up of individuals who are ready to sacrifice for the benefit of the group or the genus shall be more successful during evolution than those which are made up of egotistical individuals. However, the point, which is not explained in this theory, is how the societies which can sacrifice may maintain this characteristic. A single egotistical individual who may come up in such a society should be able to transfer its selfish characteristics to the later generations, since he is not going to sacrifice himself. Another vague point is that if evolution happens at the level of societies, what should the dimension of this society be? Should it be the family, herd, genus or class? Even if there is an evolution simultaneously at more than one level, what will be the result when interests are in conflict[3]?

As we can see, it is not possible to explain the sense of sacrifice in living beings and the social systems based on this sense with the theory of evolution, that is, by assuming that living creatures have come into being by chance.

Can the Ants Be Doormen?

When we analyze the details of the system in the ant colonies, we feel the power of the invisible will, which establishes and governs this system, in a more concrete way. Now let us take a look at these details.

The connections to the outer world of the ant nests are usually via a small hole large enough for an ant to go through. Passing through these holes is by "permission". There are ants within the colony whose numbers are not very many with the duty of "serving as a doorman".

"The doormen" serve as live plugs with the shapes of their heads fitting right in the entrance opening. Furthermore, the colour and design of their heads are the same as that of the tree barks in the close surrounding. The doorman sits for hours at the entrance hole and permits entry only to these ants that he detects as belonging to his own colony[4].

This means that the idea of keeping a doorman to guard the buildings has been put into practice, before men, by doorman ants, who cover the entrance with the strongest part of their bodies, who also camouflage themselves and who do not let in those who do not say the right "password".

It is quite obvious that that the head of the doorman ant that we mentioned above fits right into the hole, that its colour and patterns conform to the environment, and that it does not let in anybody that it does not know, cannot be up to its own will. There certainly is an owner of intellect who has designed the

In these drawings, we see the doorman ants with their special shaped heads.

body of the ant in this form and who inspires the job it is doing. To say that the ant can figure out these duties on its own and serves as a doorman without running out of patience and without giving up, would certainly not be a sensible explanation.

Let us think: Why would an ant want to be a doorman? If it had a choice, why would it pick the job, which is the most cumbersome and that requires the most sacrifice? If it did have such a chance, it would certainly pick a job that would provide it with the most comfortable environment and the best service. The choice, in fact, has come about with the determination of Allah. And the doorman ant performs its duties in full obedience. Only the creator of the ants may have designed such a perfect colony life to show the striking side of His art and given particular duties to the ant colony which abides by this system.

According to the theory of evolution, however, the ants should be developing in every respect and they should be trying to get into a caste where they could live a lot more comfortably. However, the doorman ants make no effort in this direction and they perform their inspired jobs faultlessly throughout their entire lives.

Expert Ants

The organization, specialization in certain fields, and communications in the ant world is almost as successful as among human beings. This is true to such an extent that human beings are patterning their systems today on the harmonious system of the ants. The excerpt below illustrates this point:

> Computer experts today are trying to reproduce in laboratories the collective behaviour forms of ants in robots. Instead of very advanced programmes, they are focusing on robots that cooperate devising between themselves on the basis of "simple" information elements. In these studies, the basic principle is the same. Instead of forming a highly advanced robot, the intention is to develop a herd of robots that are less "intelligent" but which will undertake the most "complex" tasks, just as the ants do in the ant colony... These robots will not be very advanced from the point of "intelligence" when taken one by one, but they will achieve the division of labour by collective action motivation. This will be possible because they will have the capacity to exchange the simplest information

with each other. The life and cooperation in the ant colony has also influenced NASA... The organization is planning to send many "ant robots" for research on the planet Mars instead of a single advanced robot. Thus, even if some of them are destroyed, the surviving members of the team will be able to complete their tasks[5].

Let us now take a look at an interesting example from the world of "expert ants".

Ants are beings that can only live in groups. They cannot survive alone.

How Does Living in a Group Affect Ants?

The most obvious example of cooperation among ants is in the behaviour of a worker ant species called *Lasius emarginatus*. The individuals of this species have interesting affiliations with each other. The activities of four worker ants belonging to the group that works with earth go on when they are separated from the big group. However, when there is a substance, like glass or stone in between which prevents them from seeing each other, their rate of work slows down.

Another example is that when the fire ants are separated from their groups by a thin barrier, they try to reach the other members of their colony by piercing this obstruction.

Many variations occur also in the behaviour of ants when the number of individuals in the group changes. When the number of ants in the nest increases, it is observed that the activity of each one of the individuals also proportionally increases. When the worker ants come together as a group, they get together, calm down and spend less energy. It has been determined that as the population increases in some ant species, there is a drop in the amount of oxygen spent.

What all these examples show us is that ants cannot survive on their own. These small creatures have been created with characteristics that allow them to live only in groups or even colonies. And this proves to us how out of touch with reality are the claims by the evolutionists with regard to the socializing process of ants. It is impossible for the ants to have been living alone when they were first created and to have socialized later on to form colonies. It would have been impossible for an ant facing such an environment to have survived. It would have had to reproduce, to build a nest for itself and its larvae, to feed both itself and its family, be a doorman, be a soldier and also a worker who took care of the larvae... We cannot claim that all these jobs requiring an extensive division of labour could have been performed once upon a time by a single ant or even a few ants. Furthermore, it is impossible to think that they worked hard towards socialization while performing these mundane tasks.

What is deduced from all this is the following: Ants are creatures who have been living under a social system and in groups since the day they were first created. This in turn is proof that ants have come into existence in one single moment with all their characteristics intact and, if we wish to phrase it better, that they have been "created".

A Model Headquarters

Let us expand a little the example of an army that we gave previously. Just think that you arrived at an army headquarters that is enormously large, but in which there is complete order. It looks as if you cannot go inside, because the security guards at the gates do not let in anybody they do not know. The building is protected with a security system that is strictly supervised.

Let us just assume that you found a way of getting in. Various systematic and dynamic activities will catch your attention inside, for thousands of soldiers are performing their duties in a strictly orderly fashion. When you search for the secret of this order, you notice that the building has been designed in a form entirely suitable for the inhabitants to work in. There are special departments for each job and these departments are designed so that the soldiers can work in the easiest manner. For instance, the building has floors underground, but the department which requires the sun's energy is located where it may get sunlight at the widest possible angle. And the departments which have to be in constant touch with each other are constructed very close to each other so that access would be facilitated. The warehouses where the surplus materials are stored are designed as a separate department in one side of the building. The warehouses where such requirements are kept are comfortable, accessible locations and there is a wide space right at the centre of the building where everybody may gather.

The features of the headquarters are not limited to these. The building is heated uniformly in spite of its vastness. The temperature stays constant all day long thanks to an extremely advanced central heating system. Another reason for this is the building's extremely effective external insulation against all weather conditions.

If the question of how and by whom this type of headquarters was designed was asked, everybody would say that it is by superior technology and by a professional team work. Such a headquarters building can only be built by people who have a certain level of education, culture, intellect and logic.

However, this headquarters building is actually an ant's nest. (please see p. 27)

To accumulate the required information to build such type of a headquarters building would take quite a long part of human life. However, an ant coming out of the egg knows its duty at that moment and starts work without losing any time. This shows that ants possess this information before they are born. All this information has been inspired in the ants at the time of their creation by Allah, the Almighty Who created them.

In the picture above, we can see the underground city ants have built in the roots of a tree. In time, the roots of the tree have been damaged and the tree has fallen to reveal this secret city.

1. Air Defence System: When the greatest enemies of ants, birds, approach the nest, some of the fighters turn their bellies upward in the opening of the nest and spurt acid towards the birds.

2. Greenhouse: In this chamber looking south, the eggs of the queen ant mature. The temperature of the chamber is constant at 38° C.

3. Main entrance and side entrances: These entrances are guarded by doorman ants. In time of danger, they close the doors with their flat heads. When other inhabitants of the colony wish to enter through the door, they tap on the doorman ant's head with their antennae with a special rhythm and the doorman ant opens up the entrance. If they forget this rhythm, the guards kill them right there and then.

4. Ready-made chambers: If ants find an old nest where they build their nest, they also use those chambers of the old nest which have maintained their shapes. Thus, they gain significant time in completion of the structure.

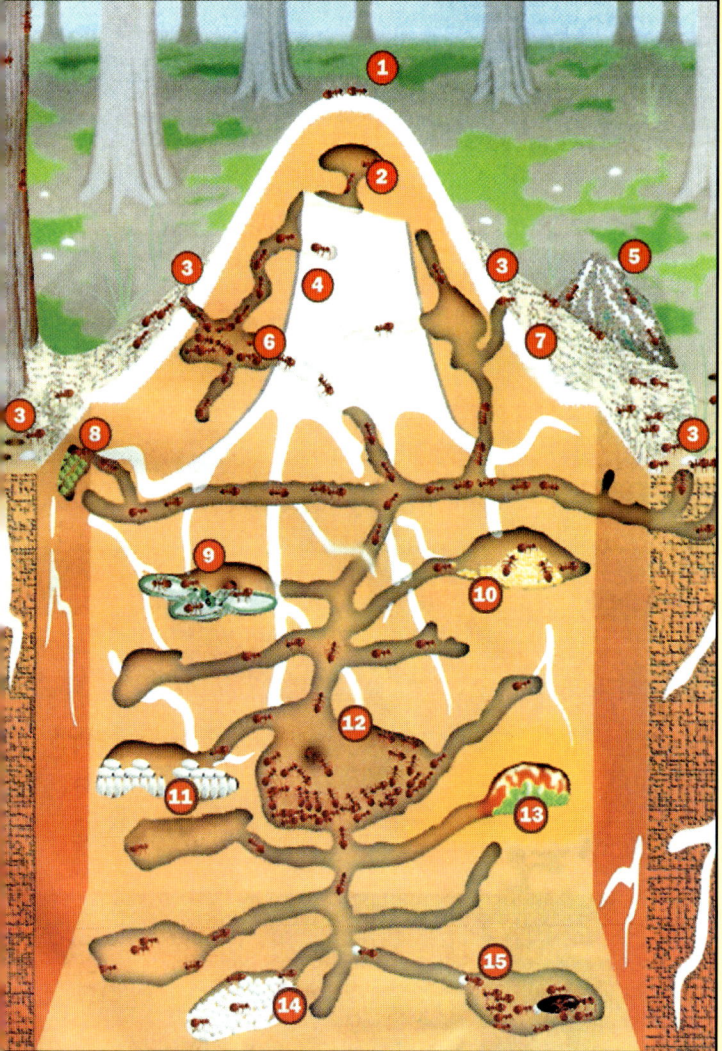

5. Storage cemetery: Ants put the non-consumed grain shells they collect and the bodies of other dead ants into these rooms.

6. Guards chamber: The soldier ants located here are in a state of alarm round the clock. When they sense the slightest danger, they swing into action.

7. Exterior insulation: This insulation, made up of pieces of branches and twigs, provides shelter for the nest against heat, cold and rain. Whether the insulation layer is decreased or not is constantly supervised by worker ants.

8. Nursing chamber: Nursing ants produce a sweet fluid from their abdomens. Raiser ants pierce their bellies by means of their antennae and utilize this fluid.

9. Meat depot: Insects, flies, crickets and enemy ants are stored in this depot after being killed.

10. Grain depot: Miller ants bring large pieces of grain in the form of small tablets here, to utilize them as bread in winter.

11. Childcare for larvae: Nurse ants use their saliva, which has antibiotic properties, to protect baby ants from disease.

12. Wintering room: Ants who hibernate, starting at the beginning of November and waking up in May, spend the long winter season here. When they wake up, they clean this room as their first duty.

13. Central heating department: Mixing of leaf pieces and twig bits here produces a certain heat. This keeps the nest temperature up to between 20 and 30 degrees.

14. Brooding room: Eggs of the queen mother are stored in this chamber in the order they are laid. Then, when the time comes, they are picked up from here and taken to the greenhouse.

15. Royalty room: The queen mother lays her eggs here. Assistants who continuously feed her and clean the chamber stay with her.[6]

Self Organization in Ants

There is no leader, planning, or programming in the world of ants. And the most important point is that there is no chain of command as we mentioned before. The most complex duties in this society are carried out without skipping a beat due to an immensely advanced self-organization. Consider the following example:

When food shortages occur in the colony, the worker ants are im-

In the first stage of nest building, members of the colony open a tiny hole, then expand into a labyrinth of chambers. In most of these sections, there are fungus gardens. These gardens fill the chambers, which are located near the surface. Larger, deeper pits hold decomposing plant detritus and waste. A few of these pits, oddly, contain more soil than organic matter, as if a soil cover is needed for especially noxious waste. Hot air rises from these refuse chambers. Cool, oxygen-rich air is drawn into the nest. Openings directly above the nest are used only for excavation and ventilation. Cavernous perimeter tunnels form a beltway some 7.5 meters from the nest.
The most important point here is that this metropolis has been constructed by ants who have not taken any architectural or agricultural courses whatsoever.

mediately transformed into "feeder" ants and they start feeding others with the food particles in their reserve stomachs, and when there is surplus food in the colony, they shed this identity and again become worker ants.

The sacrifice displayed here truly is at an advanced level. While human beings have not succeeded in fighting hunger in the world, the ants have found a practical solution to this problem: to share everything, including their food. Yes, this is a real example of sacrifice. Giving without hesitation everything it owns including its food to the next ant, so that it may survive, is just one of the examples of sacrifice in nature which the theory of evolution cannot manage to explain.

There is no overpopulation problem for ants. While today, the metropolises of man are becoming hard to live in due to migration, lack of infrastructure, misallocation of resources and unemployment, ants can manage their underground cities, with a population of 50 million in a fantastically orderly fashion, without the feeling that anything is lacking. Each ant immediately adapts to changes occurring in its environment. For such a thing to occur, the ants must have certainly been programmed physically and psychologically.

For the emergence of such extremely well organized systems, there has to be a "master will" to give them the inspiration to do their work and to give them orders. Otherwise, great chaos would ensue rather than order. And this master will pertains to Allah, Who owns everything, Who is Almighty, Who directs all living beings and orders them by inspiration.

The fact that ants perpetually strive without any consideration of benefit, is proof that they are acting on the inspiration of a certain "supervisor". The verse below fully confirms that Allah is the master and supervisor of everything and that every living creature acts on His inspiration:

I have put my trust in Allah, my Lord and your Lord. There is no living being He does not hold by the forelock and inspect! My Lord is on a straight path. (Surah Hud: 56)

COMMUNICATION IN SOCIETY

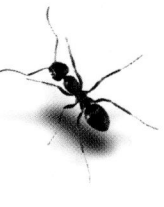

The Qur'an supplies an interesting piece of information when talking about Prophet Sulayman's armies and mentions that there is an advanced "communications system" among the ants. The verse is as follows:

> **Then, when they reached the valley of the ants, an ant said, 'Ants! Enter your dwellings so that Sulayman and his troops do not crush you unwittingly.' (Surat an-Naml: 18)**

The scientific research made on ants in this century has shown that there is an incredible communications network among these creatures. In an article published in the National Geographic magazine, this point is explained:

> Huge and tiny, an ant carries in her head multiple sensory organs to pick up chemical and visual signals vital to colonies that may contain a million or more workers, all of which are female. The brain contains half a million nerve cells; eyes are compound; antennae act as nose and fingertips. Projections below the mouth sense taste; hairs respond to touch.[7]

Even if we do not notice it, the ants have quite a different method of communication in virtue of their sensitive sensing organs. They employ these sense organs at every moment of their lives, from finding their prey to following each other, from building their nests to fighting. They have a communication system which astonishes us, as human beings with intellect, with their 500,000 nerve cells squeezed into their bodies of 2 or 3 millimetres. What we should keep in mind here is that the half a million nerve cells and the complex communication system mentioned above belongs to an ant which in bulk is almost one millionth of a human being.

In research done on social creatures like ants, bees and termites, who live in colonies, the responses of these animals in the communication process are listed under several main categories: Taking up alarm positions, meeting, cleaning, liquid food exchange, grouping, recognition, caste detection...[8]

The ants, who constitute an orderly social structure with these various responses, lead a life based on mutual news exchange and they have no difficulty in achieving this correspondence. We could say that ants, with their impressive communication system, are hundred percent successful on subjects that human beings sometimes cannot resolve nor agree upon by talking (e.g. meeting, sharing, cleaning, defence, etc.).

News Exchange Between Groups Of Ants

First, scout ants go to food source that has been newly discovered. Then they call other ants by a liquid they secrete in their glands called pheromone(*). When the crowd round the food gets bigger, this pheromone secretion issues the workers a limit again. If the piece of food is very small or far away, the scouts make an adjustment in the number of ants trying to get to the food by issuing signals. If a nice piece of food is found, the ants try harder to leave more traces thus more ants

---

(*) PHEROMONES: Is composed of the words "pher" – carrying, and "hormone" – hormone and it means "hormone carriers". Pheromones are signals used between members of the same species and they are usually produced in special glands to be spread around.

Communication by pheromones is widespread among insects. Pheromone acts as a tool of sexual attraction between females and males. The type which is analyzed most is the one used by moths as the substance of mating. A female gypsy moth may influence male moths few kilometres away by producing a pheromone called "disparlure". Since the male is able to sense a few hundred molecules of the signaling female in just one milliliters of air, disparlure is effective even when dispersed over a very large area.

Pheromones play an important role in insect communications, the ants using pheromones as tracers to show the way to food sources. When a honey bee stings, not only does it leave its needle in the skin of its victim, but it also leaves a chemical that calls the other honey bees to attack. Similarly, worker ants of many species secrete pheromones as an alarm substance to be used when threatened by an enemy; the pheromone is dispersed in the air and gathers other workers. If these ants meet the enemy, they also produce pheromones, thus the signal either increases or decreases depending upon the nature of the danger.

from the nest come to the aid of the hunters. Whatever happens, no problems arise in the consumption of the food and its transportation to the nest, because what we have here is perfect "team work".

Another example relates to the explorer ants who migrate from one nest to another. These ants advance towards the old nest from the newly found nest by leaving a trace behind. Other workers examine the new nest and if they are convinced, they also start leaving their own pheromones (chemical traces) on top of the old trace. Therefore, the ants going between the two nests increase in number and these prepare the nest. During this work, the worker ants do not stay idle. They set up a certain organization and division of labour between themselves. The tasks assumed group-wide by the ants who detect the new nest are as follows:

1. Acting as gatherers in the new area.
2. Coming to the new area and keeping watch.
3. Following the guards to receive the meeting instruction.
4. Making a detailed survey of the area.

Of course, we cannot take it for granted without pondering at all that this perfect action plan has been in practice by the ants since day one of their existence, because the division of labour required by such a plan may not have been applied by individuals who thought only of their own lives and interests. Then the following question comes to mind: "Who has been inspiring this plan in the ants for millions of years and who ensures its application?" Naturally, great intellect and power are needed for the incredibly superior group communication required by this action plan. The truth of the matter is obvious. Allah, the Creator of all living beings and possessor of infinite wisdom, shows us the way to being able to comprehend His power by displaying to us this systematic world of the ants.

Chemical Communications

All of the communication categories listed above may be grouped under the heading of: "Chemical Signals". These chemical signals play the most important role in the organization of ant colonies. Semiochemicals is the general name given to the chemicals the ants utilize for the purpose of establishing communication. Basically, there are two kinds of semiochemicals: Their names are pheromones and allomones.

Allomone is a material used for inter-genus communication. Yet pheromone, as explained before, is a chemical signal which is mostly used within a genus and, when secreted by an ant, can be perceived by another as a smell. This chemical is thought to be produced in the endocrine glands. When an ant secretes this fluid as a signal, the others get the message by way of smell or taste and respond. The research done on ant pheromones has revealed that all signals are secreted in accordance with the needs of the colony. Also, the concentration of the pheromone secreted by the ants varies in terms of the urgency of the situation.[9]

As one can see, an in-depth knowledge of chemistry is needed to manage the tasks performed by the ants. We human beings can resolve the chemicals the ants produce only by tests we perform in laboratories, plus we go through years of education to be able to do this. Yet ants can secrete these whenever they need to, and have been doing so since the day they were born, and they know quite well what response to give to which secretion.

The fact that they accurately identify the chemicals right from the time they are born shows the existence of an "Instructor" who gives them chemistry education at birth. To claim the opposite would mean that the ants have learned chemistry over time and that they have started making experiments: this would be in violation of logic. The ants know these chemicals without having had any education when they were born. We cannot say that another ant or another living creature is the "teacher" of the ant either. No insect, no living creature – including human beings – has the capacity to teach ants how to manufacture chemicals and establish communication by these substances. If there is an act of teaching before birth, the only will which would be able to achieve this act is that of Allah, Who is the Creator of all living things and "the Lord (Educator)" of the heavens and earth.

Communication between ants may be established by transmission of chemical signals by way of scent or taste.

Many people do not even know the meaning of "pheromone" – something that ants secrete continuously in their daily lives. Yet, each new-born ant performs in a perfect social communication system because of these chemicals; a social communication system which leaves no room for doubting the existence of a Creator with infinite power...

Endocrine Glands

There are basically a few endocrine glands where the complex chemical reactions we have talked about so far take place. Secretions produced in six endocrine glands provide this inter-ant chemical correspondence. However, these hormones do not display the same characteristics in each species of ant; each endocrine gland has a separate function in different species of ants. Now let us take a close look at these endocrine glands:

Dufour's Glands: The hormones produced in these glands are used in commands for alarm and meeting for attack.

The Venom Sack: An extensive formic acid production takes place in the venom sack. Also the venom which is produced to be used during attack and defence is formed here. The best example of this hormone is found in the fire ant. The venom of these ants may paralyse small animals and hurt human beings.

In a forest inhabited by ants who produce formic acid, researchers found formic acid at a level that could not be explained. All theories that were set forth were proven wrong and all research done produced no results. Eventually the shared belief of the scientists developed in the following manner:

The formic acid in the forest was formed by the acid produced by evaporation of the acid produced by ants, resulting in ecological changes. That is, these micro-creatures are able to produce and, when needed, utilize acid, on a scale that can even influence the atmosphere of the region they live in without any harm coming to themselves and this perplexes the researchers.[10]

Pygidial Glands: Three different species of ants use the secretions produced by these glands as their alarm system. The large desert harvester ant transmits this hormone in the form of a strong smell and issues a panic alarm; and the Pheidole biconstricta, which is a species of ant living in south America, utilizes the secretion it produces in these glands in chemical defence and attack alarms.

Sternal Glands: The secretions here are used during colony migrations and tracking prey and in gathering the "soldiers" together. The most original function of this secretion is to lubricate the seventh abdominal area of the ant that it frequently has to rotate when spurting out venom. Thus, the turning of its body for spurting venom becomes easier. Without this gland, which is a microscopic lubricant production centre, the defence system of the ant would be inefficient.

Yet this is not so, because there is a faultless design in place: How a tiny ant would turn its body to spray venom has been established, just as it has been pre-determined where and how this lubricant needed for reducing strain while rotating this body shall be produced.

Metapleural Glands: It has been determined that the secretions from these glands are antiseptics, which protect the body surface and the nest from micro organisms. For instance, a type of acid that is a kind of antibiotic is always found in the bodies of Attas at an amount of always 1.4 micrograms. The worker ant secretes this antiseptic hormone in small quantities from time to time. Furthermore, if it is attacked, it gives out this hormone to keep the enemy away.[11]

Let us not forget that an ant does not know how to protect itself from microbes and does not even know of the existence of the microbes. Yet, its body produces the drug against its enemies without its knowing. The

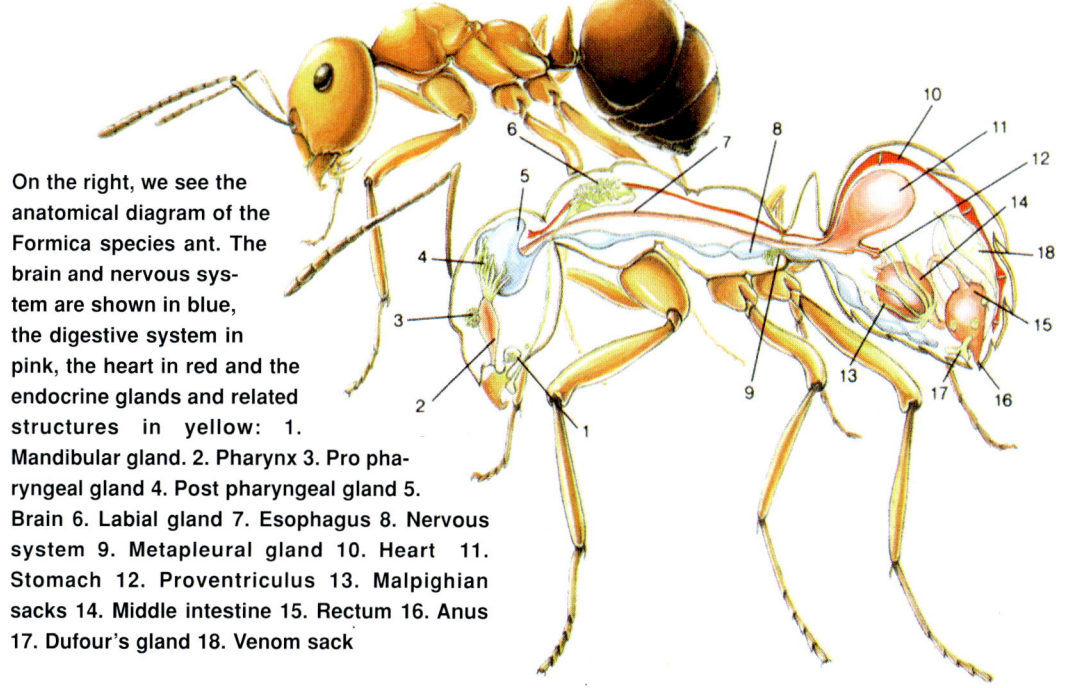

On the right, we see the anatomical diagram of the Formica species ant. The brain and nervous system are shown in blue, the digestive system in pink, the heart in red and the endocrine glands and related structures in yellow: 1. Mandibular gland. 2. Pharynx 3. Pro pharyngeal gland 4. Post pharyngeal gland 5. Brain 6. Labial gland 7. Esophagus 8. Nervous system 9. Metapleural gland 10. Heart 11. Stomach 12. Proventriculus 13. Malpighian sacks 14. Middle intestine 15. Rectum 16. Anus 17. Dufour's gland 18. Venom sack fact that there is always an antiseptic hormone in the body of the ant in an amount of 1.4 micrograms is a detail which has been worked out with great precision. Because He Who created the ant is the One Who caters for all the needs of all the living beings He created in the greatest detail, and who is indeed "Gracious".

As demonstrated, all endocrine glands mentioned in this chapter are units that have vital functions for the ants. A lack of or the insufficient functioning of any of these has adverse influences on all of the social and physical life of the ant. In fact, it makes it impossible for it to stay alive.

> **Gracious is Allah to His servants: He gives sustenance to whom He pleases: and He is the Most Strong, the Almighty.**
> **(Surat ash-Shura: 19)**

This demolishes absolutely the claims of the theory of evolution, because evolution claims that living beings have developed in stages and that starting from a primitive form, they have become more advanced gradually as a result of a series of beneficial coincidences. This would mean that the ants during the previous stages did not have part of the physiological characteristics they have today and that they acquired these later on. However, all the secretions of the ants we discussed above are vital and without them it is impossible for an ant species to survive.

The conclusion from all this is that the ants were created at the outset with these endocrine glands and vital functions. That is, they did not wait for the development of the necessary endocrine glands for hundreds of thousands of years in order to have a defence and communications system. Had that been so, it would have been impossible for the ant genus to have survived. The only explanation is that the first ant species which existed on earth did so in the same complete and perfect form as it is in today. A perfect system cannot be other than the artwork of an intelligent designer. If we are able today to talk about an ant society with a population of billions, then we must admit that a single Creator has created these all at once.

The Identity Card of Ants: Colony Scent

We had mentioned previously that the ants can recognize each other and distinguish their relatives and friends from the same colony. Zoologists are still investigating how the ants can recognize their relatives. While man cannot distinguish between the few ants he may come across, let us see now how these creatures who are so completely alike can recognize each other.

An ant can easily detect if another ant is from its own colony or not. A worker ant touches the body of the other ant to recognize it, in case it enters the nest. It can immediately distinguish between the ones who belong to the colony and the ones who do not by virtue of the special colony scent it carries. If the ant who enters the nest is a stranger, the hosts attack this uninvited guest cruelly. The inhabitants of the nest bite the stranger's body with their powerful jaws and make it helpless by the formic acid, citronellal and other toxic substances that they secrete.

If the guest is from the same species but from a different colony, they can understand that too. In this case the guest ant is accepted in the nest. However, the guest ant is given less food until it acquires the scent of the colony.[12]

How Is the Scent of Colonies Obtained?

The source of the scents that ensure recognition by ants from the same colony is not fully explained. However, as far as it has been discovered, ants use hydrocarbons for the scent distinguishing process among themselves.

The experiments performed have shown that ants who belong to the same species, but to different colonies, recognize each other by hydrocarbon differences. An interesting experiment was carried out to understand this. First, the workers in one colony were washed with fluids carrying the scent of the ants belonging to the same species as themselves, but from other colonies. It was observed that while the other ants of the colony displayed aggressive behaviour to the ones who took a fluid bath, the other colony whose scent was used for the experiment did not react against these workers.[13]

Has the Scent of Colonies Evolved?

A very significant point which has to be carefully considered with regard to the scent of colonies is the matter of evolution. How do the evolution mechanisms explain the fact that ants, or members of other insect colonies (bees, termites etc.) can recognize their friends by their exclusive pheromones?

People who try to defend the theory of evolution in spite of all kinds of impossibilities claim that pheromones are the result of natural selection (The preservation of beneficial changes occurring in living beings and elimination of harmful ones). Yet, this is out of the question for any insect species including ants. A most striking example on this point is the honey bee. When a honey bee stings its enemy, it produces a pheromone for notifying the other bees that there is danger. However, it dies right after this. In this case, this means that this pheromone is produced only once. Then, it is impossible for such a "beneficial change" to be transferred to the following generations and become propagated by natural selection. This explanation indicates that it is impossible for the chemical communications between insect species that have the caste system to have evolved by the method of natural selection. This characteristic of the insects, which rebuts the theory of natural selection completely, demonstrates once more that the One who establishes the communications network among them is the One "who creates them for the first time."

Call of the Ants

Ants have a level of self-sacrifice which is very advanced and, due to this characteristic, they always invite their friends to each source of food they find and they share their food with them.

In such situations, the ant that discovers the food source directs the others to it. The following method is used for this: The first explorer ant that finds the food source fills its crop and returns home. As it returns, it drags its tummy on the ground at short intervals and leaves a chemical signal. Yet its invitation does not end there. It tours around the ant hill for a short while. It does this between three to sixteen times. This motion ensures contact with its nest mates. When the explorer wishes to return to the food source, all its mates that it has met wish to follow it. Yet only the friend which is in the closest antenna contact may accompany it outside. When the scout reaches the food, it returns immediately to the hill and assumes the part of the host. The scout and its other worker friend are joined to each other via continuous sense signals and the pheromone hormone on the surfaces of their bodies.

Ants may reach their target by following the track that goes to the food, even when there is no inviting ant. Because of the track that successful explorers leave from the food to the nest, when the explorer comes to the nest and does the "rock dance", its nest mates reach the food source without any help from the inviter.

Another interesting side to ants is their production of many chemical compounds to be used in the process of invitation, each one with a different task. It is not known why so many different chemicals are used to be gathered around the food source but, as far as one can tell, the diversity of such substances make sure that tracks are different from each other. Apart from these, ants transmit different signals when sending messages, and the intensity of each signal is different from the others. They increase the intensity of the signal when the colony gets hungry, or when new nest areas are needed.

This solidarity among ant societies at such a high level may be regarded as behaviour that is worth considering and that can be taken as an example for men. Compared to human beings who unhesitatingly violate the rights of other individuals on account of their own interests – which are all they think about - the tremendously self-sacrificing ants are much more ethical.

It is in no way possible to explain the totally unselfish behaviour of ants, in terms of the theory of evolution. This is because evolution assumes that the only rule existing in nature is the fight for survival and the accompanying conflict. Yet, the behavioural characteristics that ants and many other types of animals display disprove this and show the reality of sacrifice.

The theory of evolution, in fact, is nothing other than an attempt by those who wish to legalize their own selfishness to ascribe this selfishness to the whole of nature.

Touch Function in Chemical Communications

The communications by ants by touching each other with their antennas in maintaining intra-colony organization proves that there is in use an "antenna language" in its fullest sense.

The antenna signals created by touching in ants are used for various purposes like commencement of dinner, invitations and social meetings where nest mates get to know each other. For instance, in one type of worker ant species living in Africa, workers first touch antennas when they meet each other. Here, "antenna shaking" means just a salute and an invitation to the nest.

This invitation motion is very obvious in certain ant species (*Hypoponera*). When a pair of workers meet face to face, the inviting ant tilts its head to the side 90 degrees and touches the bottom and top parts of the head of its friend with its antennas. The invitee ant responds the same way.[14] When the ants touch the bodies of their nest mates, the goal is not to give them information but to obtain information by detecting the chemicals they secrete. One ant taps lightly on the body of its nest mate and touches strongly with its antenna. When it gets close to its nest mate, its goal here is to bring the chemical signals as close as possible to the other. As a result, it will be able to detect and follow the scent path its friend has just left and reach the food source.

The most striking example that may be set forth for communication by touch is an ant's feeding another ant with the food it has kept in its crop by getting it out of its mouth by a short touch. In an interesting test made on this subject, various parts of the bodies of worker ants of the *Myrmica* and *Formica* species were stimulated by human hair and were thus successfully prompted to bring liquid food out of their mouths. The most sensitive ant was the one which had just eaten and was looking for a nest mate with which to share what it had eaten. Researchers noted that certain insects and parasites were aware of such tactics and they were having themselves fed by practising this method. What the insect had to do to attract the ant's attention was just to touch the ant's body slightly with its antenna and its front leg. Then the touched ant would share its meal, even if the creature in contact with it is of a different type.[15]

The ability of an ant to understand what the other one wants by a short antenna contact shows that the ants may, in a sense, "speak" among themselves. How this "antenna language" used among ants is learned by all ants is another subject to think about. Are they undergoing training on this subject? To talk about the existence of such training, we must also talk about the existence of a superior Almighty Who provides it. Since it cannot be the ants who can provide such a training, this Almighty is Allah Who, by way of inspiration, teaches all ants a language with which to communicate.

The sharing behaviour practised among ants is a specimen of self-sacrifice that cannot be explained by the theory of evolution. Some evolutionists who see the adage "Big fish swallow small fish" as the key to life on earth are forced to withdraw such words when confronted with

Ants establishing communication with each other by touch.

such self-sacrifice as is displayed by ants. In an ant colony, instead of the "big ant" developing by eating the "small ant", it rather attempts to feed the "small ant" and make it grow. All ants are ready to accept the food - that is, the "provision" - given to them and definitely make sure to share the excess with other members of the colony.

As a result, what all these examples show us is that the ants are a society of living beings who have submitted to the will of the Creator and who act under His inspiration. Therefore, it would not be right to regard them as organisms which are totally unconscious, because they do have a consciousness which reflects the will of their Creator. Indeed, Allah draws attention in the Qur'an to this interesting fact and notifies us that all living things are, in fact, a community among themselves, that is, they live under a Divine order and in accordance with inspiration.

There is not an animal that lives on the earth, nor a being that flies on its wings, but forms communities like you. We have not omitted anything from the Book, and they will be gathered to their Lord. (Surat al-An'am: 38)

Communication By Sound

Communication by sound is another method used frequently by ants. Two kinds of voice production have been determined. One is the "tapping" sound and vibrations produced by hitting an obstruction, or the ground, with the body, and the other is the high notes produced by rubbing certain parts of the body against each other.[16]

The voice signal produced by hitting with the body is usually used by colonies that have tree nests. For instance, carpenter ants communicate by "playing drums". They start "playing drums" in the face of any danger approaching their nests. This danger may be a sound that causes anxiety or a touch that they feel or a suddenly developing air current. The drummer ant taps the ground with its chin and belly by rocking its body back and forth. This way, signals easily may be sent via thin barks as far away as decimetres.[17] The European carpenter ants send vibrations to their nest mates who are 20 cm or even farther away by tapping with their chins and bellies on the woodwork of rooms and corridors. It must be taken into account here that 20 cm for an ant is a distance that would correspond to 60-70 metres for a human being.

Ants are almost deaf to vibrations transmitted through air. However, they are very sensitive to sound vibrations transmitted through matter. This is a very efficient warning signal for them. When they hear it they quicken their pace, they move towards the place where the vibration comes from and they attack all moving living beings that they see around.

No disobedience to this call by any of the members of the colony is an indication of successful organization of the ant society. One must admit that even a small human society responding to an alarm call collectively, at the same time, without any exception, and without anarchy developing, is a very difficult thing in practice. Yet ants are able to do what they are ordered without losing any time and so they are able to lead their lives without interrupting the discipline within the colony even for a moment.

The production of high sounds is more complex as a system than the process of playing drums. The sound produced is created by rubbing certain parts of the body together. Ants produce this sound by rubbing together the organs at the rear of their bodies. If you get your ear close to the worker harvester ants, you may hear them produce a high pitched voice all the time.

Three major functions of voice communication have been discovered in different species. These may be listed as follows:

1. Voice communication in leaf cutter ants functions as an underground warning system. It is usually used when a portion of the colony is buried under a cave-in of the nest. Workers start moving to perform rescue excavations responding to received sound signals.

2. High pitched voices are used in some species during the mating of queens. When young queens are gathered on the ground and/or on plants for mating, and have obtained enough sperm, they produce a high pitched sound to prevent the male ant herds from catching them.

3. Yet in other species, sound is used to increase the efficiency of the pheromone produced during the gathering of the nest members to find food or new nests.[18]

Sometimes in certain species, the food searchers make it possible for other ants to surround the prey with signals they produce when they find a prey. Gathering together of the workers and getting to the prey is realized within 1-2 minutes on account of this high pitched voice. These features are a great advantage for the ant species.

For An Eye That Sees…

With their various communication methods, ants may be compared to men who can speak several foreign languages. They are able to communicate with 3-4 different languages among themselves and they are able to pursue their lives in the least problematic manner. They are able to subsist their colonies with populations of hundreds of thousands or sometimes millions, and survive all their lives without causing any confusion.

Yet this communication system we have been describing so far is just one of the miraculous features of the animal world. When we analyse both people and also all other living beings (From single-celled to multi-celled) we can discover characteristics that are different from each other, with each being a separate and individual miracle with its place in an ecological order.

For an eye that can notice all these miracles that are created around it, and a heart that can feel, it will be sufficient to look at the extraordinary communication system of the ant of millimetric dimensions to appreciate the infinite power, knowledge and wisdom of Allah Who is the sole Owner and Sovereign of all living things. In the Qur'an, Allah refers to these people who do not have this capability and who may not appreciate His might:

> **Have they not travelled about the earth and do they not have hearts to understand with or ears to hear with? It is not their eyes which are blind but the hearts in their breasts which are blind. (Surat al-Hajj:46)**

ANT SPECIES

Although all ants may seem alike, they are divided into many different species based on their lifestyles and physical attributes. These living beings in fact have approximately 8800 species. Each species also has special admirable attributes. Now, let us discuss some of these species, their lifestyles and characteristics.

Leaf Cutter Ants

The specific characteristic of the leaf cutter ants also called "atta," is their habit of transporting the leaf pieces that they cut out on their heads. The ants hide under leaves that are quite large compared to their own sizes. These they secure in their closely shut chins. Therefore, the return voyage of worker ants after a day's work presents a very interesting picture. Anyone who sees this happening would feel as if the floor of the forest were alive and walking. In rain forests their actions remove about 15 percent of leaf production.[19] The reason for their carrying leaf pieces is, of course, not protection from the sun. Ants do not utilize these leaf pieces as food either. Then, in what way do they use so many leaves?

It has been discovered that, surprisingly, Attas use these leaves in the production of mushrooms. Ants cannot eat the leaves themselves, because they do not have enzymes in their bodies that could digest the cellulose in the leaves. Worker ants make a heap of these leaf pieces after chewing them and keep them in the rooms of the nest underground. In these chambers, they raise mushrooms on the leaves. This way, they obtain the required protein from the shoots of the mushrooms.[20]

However, when Attas are removed, the garden would normally begin to deteriorate and would soon be overwhelmed by weed fungi.

Then, how can the Attas, who clean their gardens only before "planting," be protected against weed fungi? The trick of maintaining a pure fungus culture without constant weeding seems to depend upon the saliva the ants work into the compost as they chew it up. It is thought that the saliva contains an antibiotic that inhibits the growth of undesirable fungi. It probably contains a growth-promoter for the right fungus, too.[21] What one has to ponder upon is the following: How have these ants learned to cultivate mushrooms? Is it possible that one day one of the ants took a leaf in its mouth by coincidence and chewed it, and then again by chance, it placed this liquid that had become porridge-like on a dry leaf floor which, by sheer coincidence is a totally appropriate place, and other ants brought pieces of mushrooms and planted them there and, finally, the ants which had anticipated that some sort of food that they could eat would grow there, started cleaning the garden, throwing out unnecessary material, and harvesting? And then they went over and conveyed this process to the whole colony one by one? Also, why would they have carried all those leaves to their nests although they could not eat them?

Furthermore, how could these ants have created the saliva that they use while chewing the leaves for the production of mushrooms? Even it is thought that they may form this saliva, one way or the other, with what information could they produce an antibiotic in their saliva which prevents the formation of weed fungi? Does it not require having a significant knowledge of chemistry to achieve such a process? Even if they did have such knowledge - which is impossible- how could they apply it and get their saliva to have this antibiotic substance characteristic?

When one thinks about how ants could realize such a miraculous event, hundreds of similar questions come up to none of which there are any answers.

On the other hand, if a single explanatory answer could be given, all these questions would have been answered. Ants have been designed and programmed to achieve the job they are performing. The observed event is sufficient to prove that ants are born or rather caused to be born knowing farming. Such complex behavioural patterns are not phenomena which may develop in stages and with time. They are the work of a comprehensive knowledge and a supreme intellect. Thus the claims by

Due to the symbiosis of leaf cutter ants and fungi, the ants obtain the protein they need for nutrition from the mushroom buds they grow on leaves. Above we see a mushroom garden tended by ants.

1) Inside the nest, slightly smaller workers chop leaves into bits.

2) The next caste chews these bits into pulp and fertilizes with deposits of enzyme-rich fecal fluid.

3) Other ants apply the fertile leaf paste over a base of dried leaves in new chambers.

4) Another caste hauls in bits of fungus from older chambers and plants it in the leaf paste. Bits of fungus spread on the leaf paste like frost.

5) A teeming caste of dwarfs cleans and weeds the garden, then harvests the fungus for others to eat.[22]

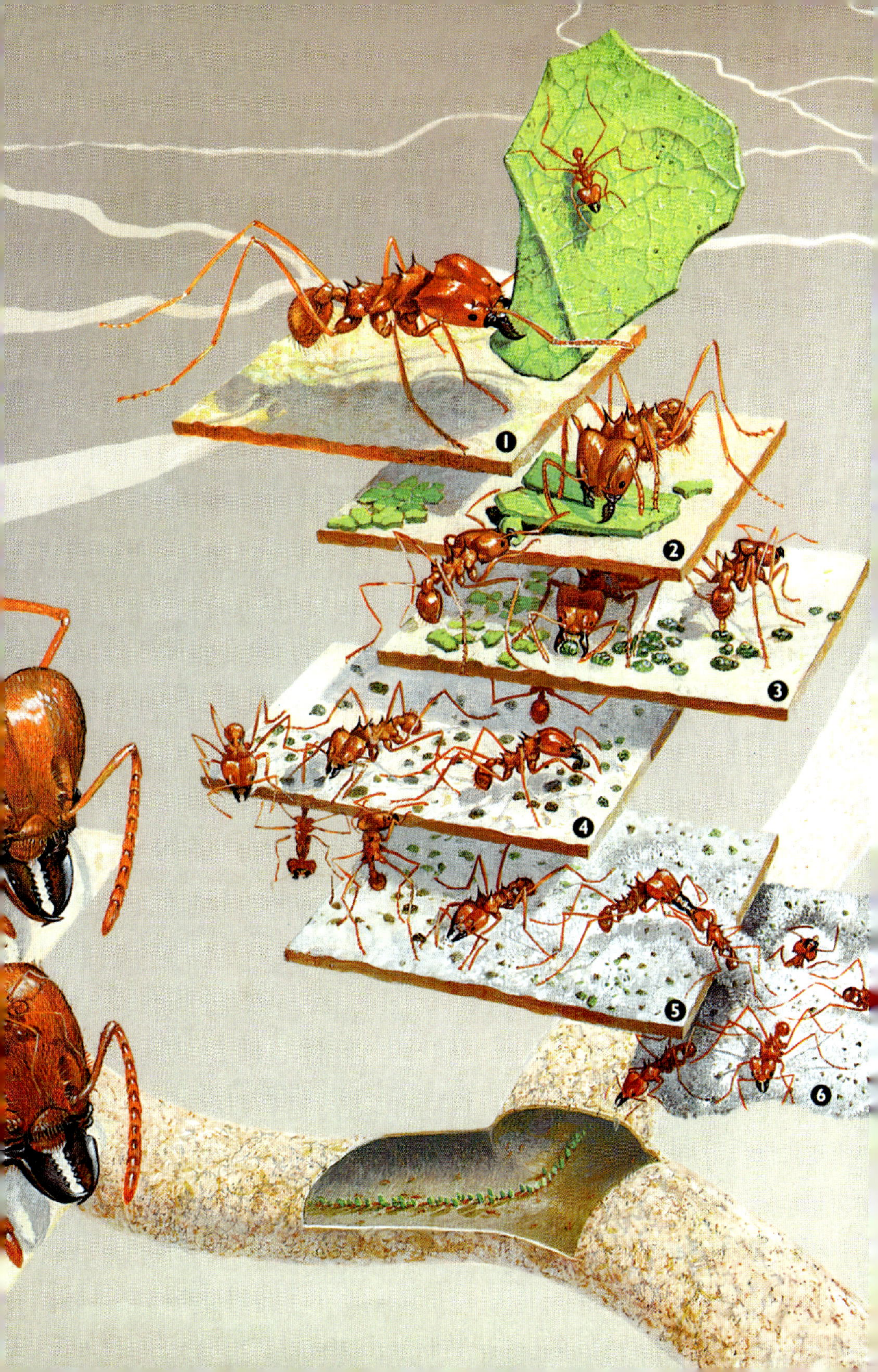
1
2
3
4
5
6

evolutionists that beneficial behaviour is selected in time and the required organs develop through mutations seem totally illogical. It is, of course, no one other than Allah who gives this knowledge to the ants from day one, and Who creates them with all these astonishing features. It is Allah who is the "Creator" (Sani). The features of the Atta ants we mention above set forth a picture we shall face frequently all throughout this book. We are talking about a living being without the ability to think, but which nevertheless achieves a great task displaying a tremendous intellect. This is hard for man to conceive of.

Then, what does this all mean?

There is only one answer and it is a simple one: If this animal has no capacity to think in order to enable it to do what it is doing, then its show of intellect, in fact, introduces us somebody else's Wisdom. The Creator Who has caused the ant to exist is letting this animal do things beyond its capacity to show His existence and superiority in His creation. The ant acts under Allah's inspiration and the intellect it displays is in fact, the Wisdom of Allah.

Leaf cutter ant on duty

Actually, a similar situation exists in the whole of the animal world. We meet creatures who display a very superior intellect, although they have neither an independent mind nor the capacity for judgement. The ant is one of the most striking of these and like other animals, acts, in fact, in accordance with the programme it has been given by the Will that trains it. It reflects the Wisdom and power of Possessor of that Will, that is, Allah.

Now, let us continue reviewing the superior skills of ants with this basic knowledge.

The Attas' Interesting Defence Methods

Medium-sized workers of the leaf cutter ant colony spend almost all their days in carrying leaves. It becomes difficult for them to protect themselves during this process, because they secure the leaves with the chins that they use for protecting themselves. Then, if they are not able to protect themselves, who does?

It has been observed that leaf cutter worker ants walk around with smaller size workers all the time. At first, it was thought that this was accidental. Then, the cause for this was researched and the finding, which was the result of a long analysis, was an astonishing example of cooperation.

Medium-sized ants, given the task of carrying leaves use an interesting defence system against a hostile type of fly. This hostile fly has chosen a special place to lay its eggs - the head portion of each ant. The maggot hatching from the egg would feed on the ant's head, eventually decapitating the ant. Without their smaller assistants, the worker ants are defenceless against this fly species that is always ready to attack. Under normal circumstances, the ants who, with their scissors like sharp jaws, are able to chase away the flies trying to land on them, cannot do this while carrying leaves.

Above we see an Atta, along with its small-sized guard, carrying a leaf.

The ant in the picture carries an extra small ant over the leaf it carries. The reason for this is to be able to be protected againt potential enemies that may attack it.

THE MIRACLE IN THE ANT

Therefore, they place another ant to defend them, on the leaf that they carry and during the attack, these small guards fight against the enemy.[23]

Highways of Attas

The road that Attas use, while carrying the leaves they cut back to home, seems like a miniature highway. Ants who crawl slowly on it collect all twigs, small gravel, grass and wild plants and put them to one side. Thus, they make a clear path for themselves. After a long period of intensive work, this highway becomes straight and smooth as if built with a special device.

The Atta colony consists of workers the size of a single grain of sand, soldiers who are many times larger and medium-sized "Marathon runners". Marathon runners run around to bring leaf pieces to the nest. These ants are so industrious that, scaled to human dimensions, each worker runs the equivalent of four-minute mile for 30-some miles (48 km.), with 500 pounds(227 kg.) slung over her shoulders.[24]

In an Atta nest, fist-sized galleries may be found that may go 6 metres deep. The miniature workers may move some 40 tons of soil while digging the many chambers of their huge nests.[25] The building of these

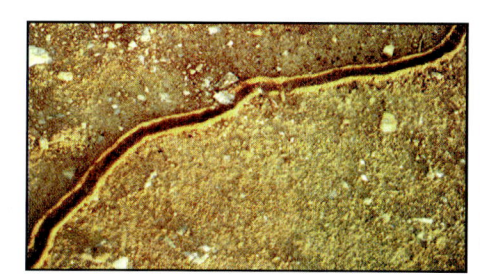

When carrying the leaves they cut, Attas clear the road they use of all kinds of twig bits, gravel and grass remnants. Thus they prepare what amounts to a "highway" for themselves.

nests in a few years by ants is comparable in difficulty and high standard of professionalism to man's construction of the Great Wall of China.

This is proof that the Attas may not be regarded as ordinary simple creatures. These ants, who are extremely hard working, are able to achieve complex tasks that a man would find difficult to do. Indeed, the only Possessor of might Who could have given them such skills is Allah. To say that they have acquired all these skills on their own and of their own accord would be illogical.

Leaf Cutting Technique of Attas

When the ant cuts the leaf with its mandibles, its whole body vibrates. Scientists have observed that this shaking fixes the leaves, thus facilitating the cutting. At the same time, the sound serves to attract other workers-all females-to the site to finish off the leaf.[26] The ant rubs two small organs on his belly to produce this vibration that may be heard as a very slight sound by human beings. This vibration is sent through the body until reaching the sickle-like mandibles of the ant. By rapidly oscillating her hind end, this ant cuts out a crescent of leaf with vibrating mandibles in much the same manner as an electric carving knife.

This technique facilitates the cutting of the leaf. Yet, it is known that such vibrations serve another purpose as well. Seeing a leaf-cutting ant attracts others to the same place because many other plants in the regions where Attas live are poisonous. The testing of each leaf by an ant being such a risky procedure, they always go to locations where others have successfully completed their tasks.

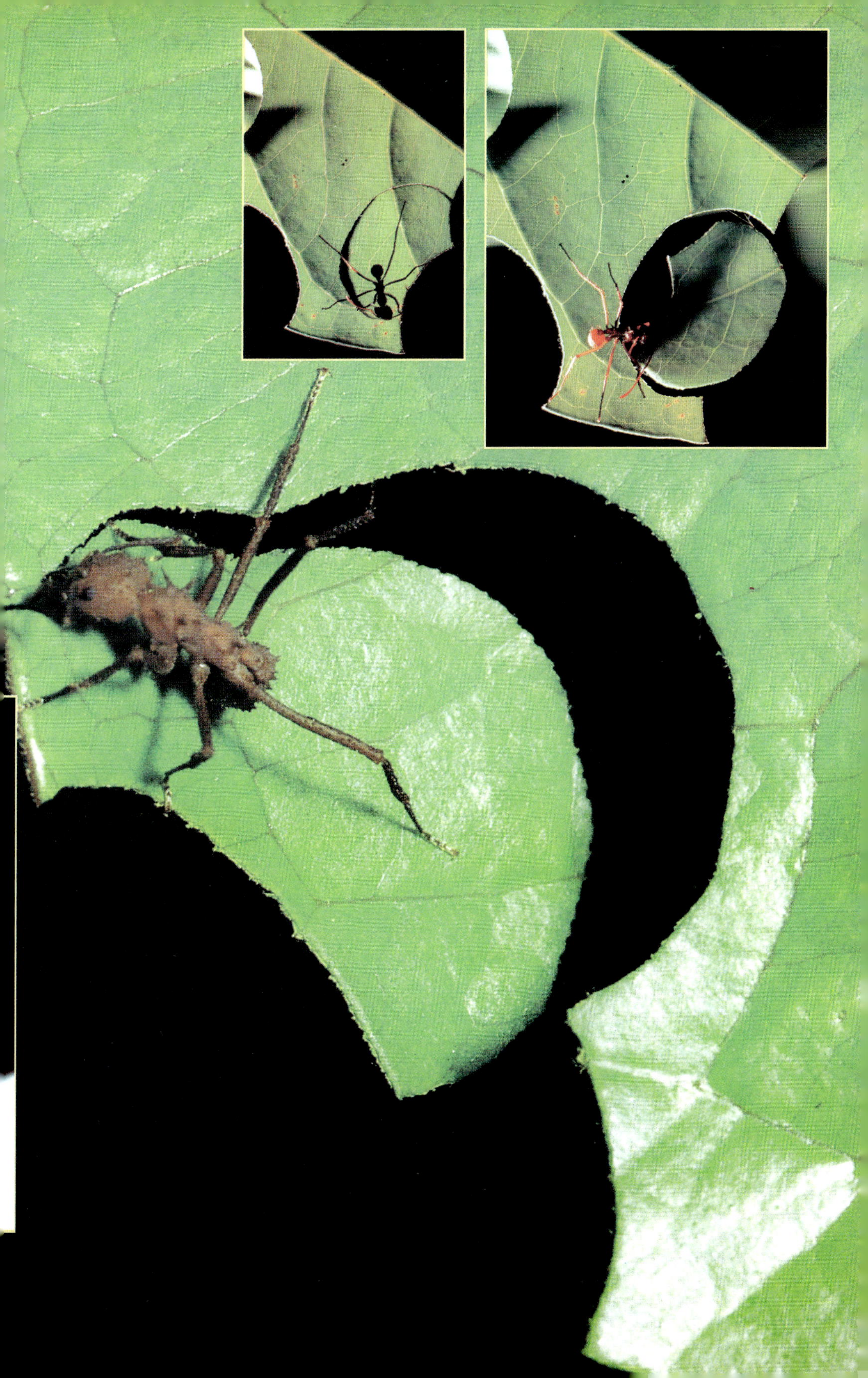

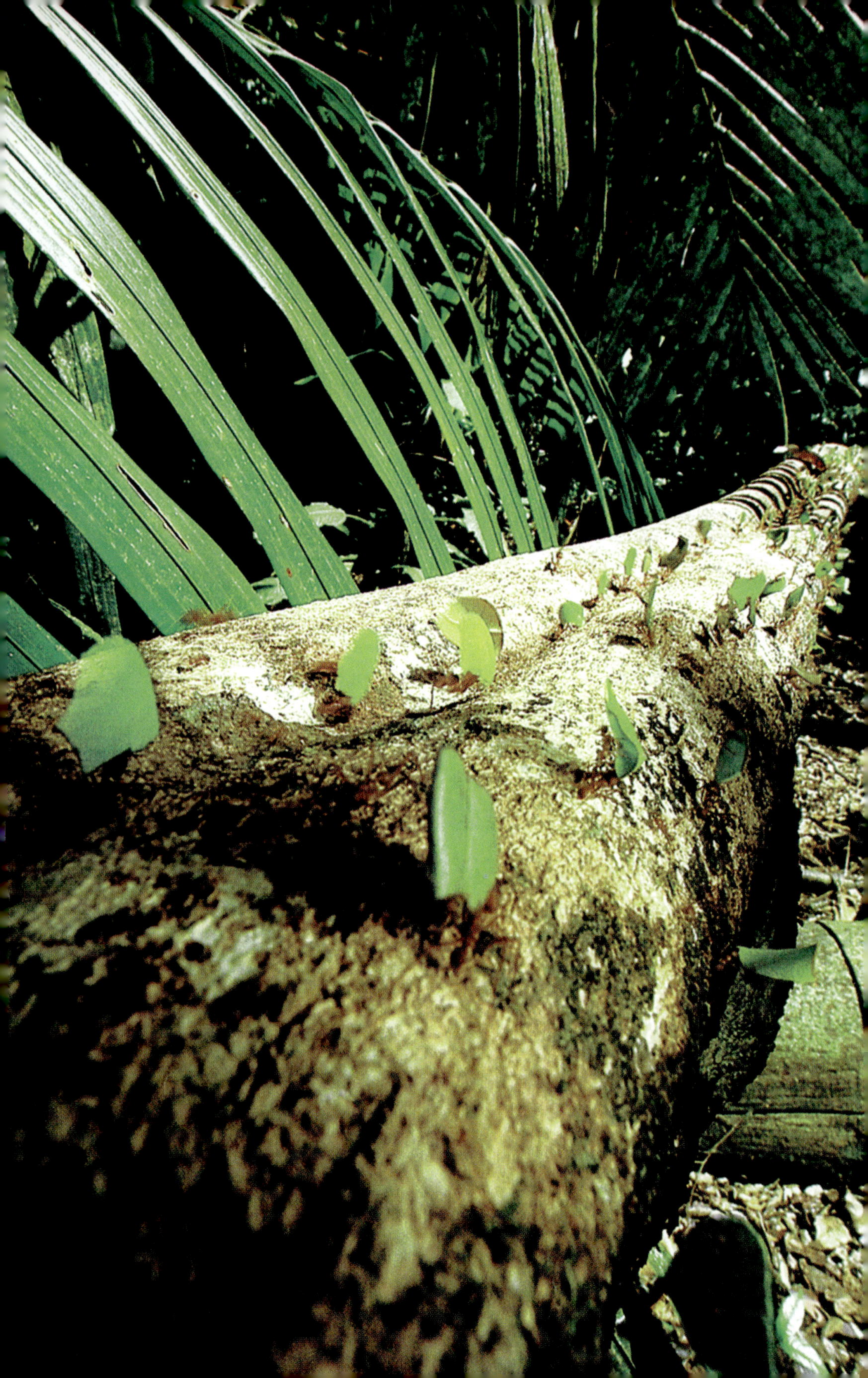

Weaver Ants

Weaver ants live in the trees building themselves nests out of leaves. By combining the leaves, they are able to form nests over a few trees, thus supporting a much larger population.

The stages of building are interesting. First, workers individually seek locations in the colony territory that are suitable for expansion. When they find a suitable branch, they disperse over the leaves of the branch and start pulling in the leaves from the sides. When an ant succeeds in bending a portion of a leaf, the workers close by also move towards it and start pulling the leaf together. If the leaf is wider than the size of the ant, or if it is necessary to pull two leaves together, the workers form a life bridge between the points to be joined. Later on, some of the ants in the chain climb on the backs of the ants beside them, thus shortening the chain, and the joining of the ends of the leaf is achieved. When the leaf takes a tent-like shape, some of the ants keep holding the leaf with their legs and jaws and others go back to the old nest and carry specially raised larvae to this region. Workers rub the larvae back and forth over the joints of the leaf, using them as a source of silk. With the silk secreted from an opening right below the mouths of the larvae, the leaves are fastened at the required locations. That is, the larvae are used as sewing machines.[27]

These larvae, raised for their silks, have larger than average silk glands, but they may be carried easily because they are smaller in size. The larvae give all their silk for the needs of the colonies instead of using them for themselves. Instead of producing silk slowly from their silk glands, they secrete silk in great quantities on a single occasion, and they do not even try to build their own cocoons. In the remaining portion of their lives, worker ants will do everything the larvae have to do for them. As is evident, these larvae live only as "silk manufacturers".[28]

How the ants could develop such cooperation has never been explained by scientists. Another unexplained point is how this behaviour emerged for the first time during this alleged term of evolution. As with the wings of the insects, the eyes of the vertebrates and other biological miracles, how such sophisticated and beneficial faculties developed by evolving from the first living beings is a phenomenon which cannot be

Phases of nest building by weaver ants... In the first phase, ants pick the right leaves on the tree they plan to settle in, and combine them by pulling from two sides. Later on, they bring their silk producing larvae, as shown at the bottom, and sew the leaves together by using them as sewing machines.

A leaf nest prepared to meet all requirements

explained by the basic principles of evolution. It is a dead end for defenders of evolution.

It would not of course, be logical to say that one day the larvae came together and said that "some of us have to produce silk to meet the needs of the whole colony, so let us adjust our weights and silk glands accordingly." That would not be a very smart theory. We, therefore, have to admit that larvae have been created knowing what to do. In other words, Allah, Who created these larvae, shaped them in such a way as is suitable for their tasks.

Harvester Ants

Some of the ants, as mentioned before, are expert "farmers". Among these, it is possible to list harvester ants, apart from the Attas we talked about before.

Harvester ants carry starchy seeds to special chambers and convert them into a form to be used in the nourishment of workers.

The feeding mechanisms of harvester ants are quite sophisticated and complex as compared to the feeding mechanisms of other types of ants. These collect seeds and keep them in specially prepared rooms. These seeds, made up of starch, are used for producing the sugar that will feed the larvae and other workers. While many ants use the seeds and kernels as food, only harvester ants have a system based on gathering seeds and processing them.

These ants collect the seeds in the growing season and store them for use in the arid season. In special rooms in the nest, they sort out the

In the chambers we see above, seeds to be used in the arid season are stored by harvester ants.

seeds from other objects mistakenly brought back. Some groups of ants stay in the nest by the hour, chewing the seeds' contents and thus producing so-called ant bread. The ants were once thought to use some learned process to convert the seeds' starch into the sugar they eat. It is now known that the abundant saliva they secrete while chewing accomplishes this transformation.[29]

The ants we speak of here have not, of course, had any education in chemistry. Neither can they anticipate that their saliva will transform the seeds they collect randomly into sugar that they can eat. Yet, the lives of these ants depend on a series of chemical transformations that they do not know about and cannot know about. When even men do not know of such a transformation process taking place in the bodies of the ants – and they have just learned the details in the last few years – how have the ants managed to be fed by this method for millenniums?

Honey Ants

Many types of ants are fed with the digestive wastes of aphids called "honey". This substance in fact bears no relation to real honey. However, the digestive waste of aphids, which have fed on plant sap, is given this name because it contains a high proportion of sugar. Thus, the workers of this species, called honey ants, collect honey from aphids, coccidae, and flowers. The ants' method of collecting honey from the aphid is very

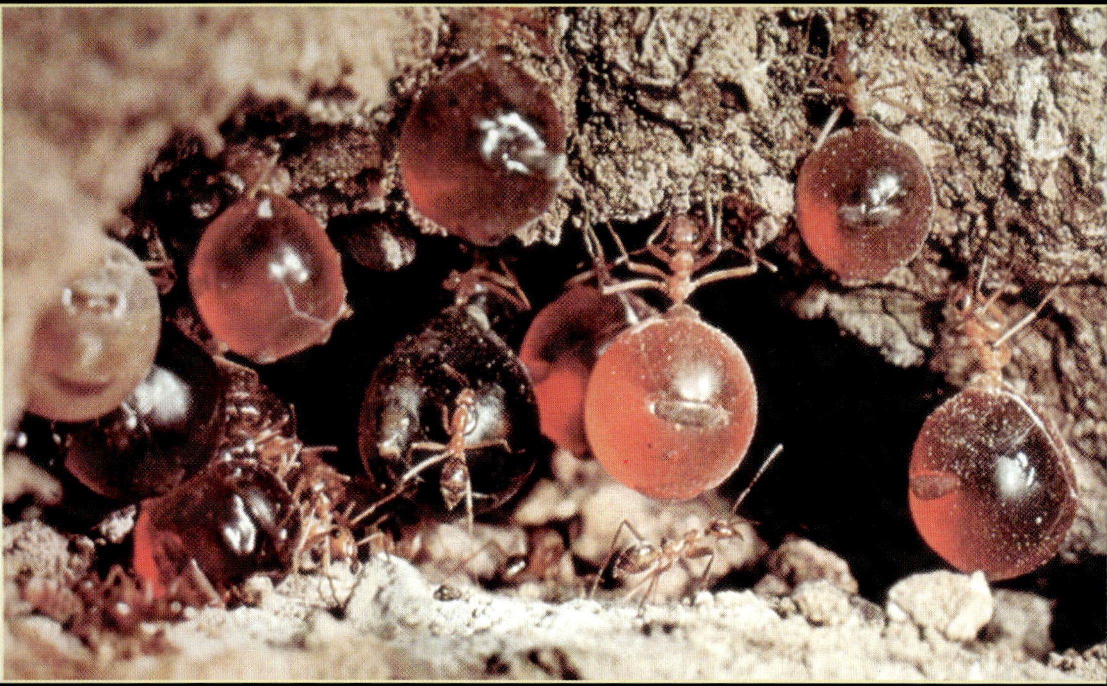

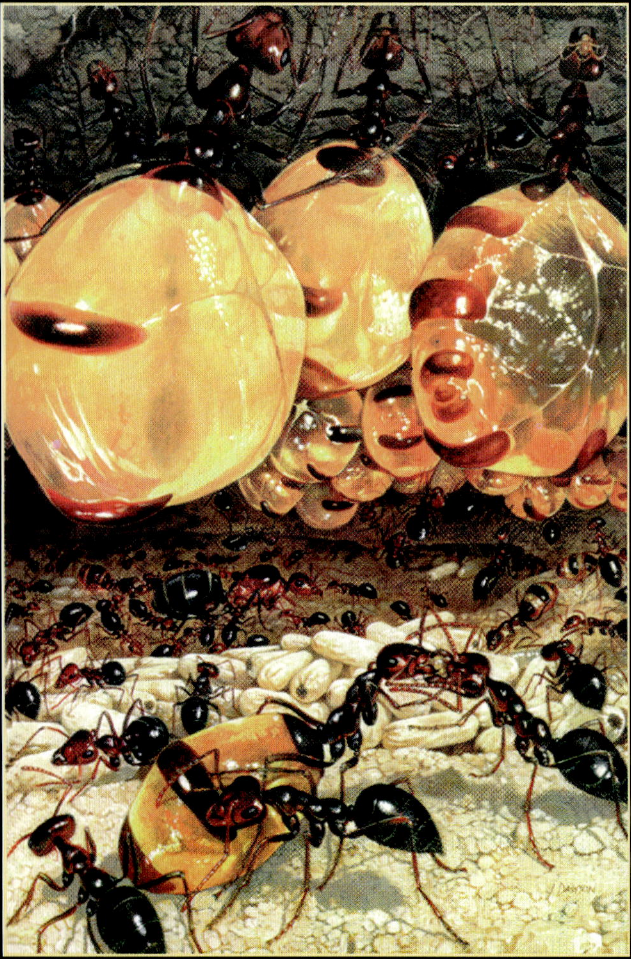

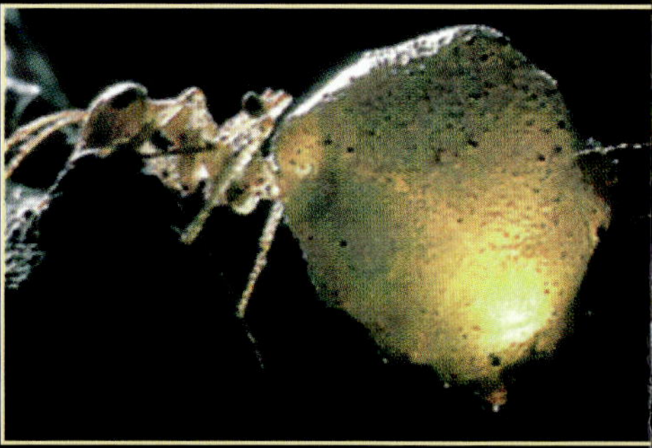

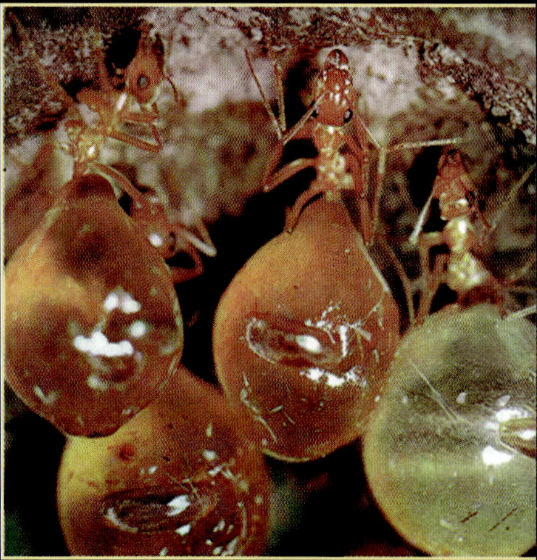

interesting. The ant approaches the aphid and starts shoving its belly. The aphid gives a drop of digestive waste to the ant. The ant starts shoving the belly of the aphid more and more to get more honey and sucks the liquid that comes out. Then how do they utilize this sugared food and what good is this food for them later on?

There is a great division of labour among honey ants in this phase. Some ants are used as "jars" to keep the nectar collected by other workers!...

In every nest, there is one queen, workers and also honey carriers. The colonies of these ants are usually located near the dwarf oak trees the workers can extract nectars from. After the workers carry the nectar, once having swallowed it, to their nests, they take it out of their mouths and pour it into the mouths of young workers who will keep the honey. These workers, nicknamed honeypots, use their own bodies to store the sweet liquid food the colony often needs to get through hard times in the desert. They are fed until they swell up to the size of blueberries. Then they dangle like amber globes from the ceilings of their chambers until called upon to regurgitate nectar to hungry sisters.[30] While attached to this ceiling, they look like a small and translucent bunch of grapes. If any of them falls down, the workers return it to its previous position right away. Honey in the honey pots weighs almost 8 times as much as an ant.

In winter, or in the arid season, ordinary workers visit the honey pots to meet their daily food demands. The worker ant places its mouth on to the "pot's" and the pot exudes a small drop of honey from its store by contracting its muscles. The workers consume this honey of high nutritional value as food in adverse seasons.

It is an interesting and awe-inspiring situation for a living being to reach a weight 8 times its own, having decided to serve as a honey pot, and to be able to live hanging from its feet without any harm coming to it. Why have they felt the need to accept such a difficult and dangerous position? Have they thought about this unique storage technique themselves and controlled their bodily developments accordingly? Just think, while a man cannot even control the slightest development in his body, how can an ant, who does not even have a brain in the real sense, do this on its own?

As shown in the picture above, honey pots that have been inflated by storing food look like grapes.

Honey ants display behavior that the evolution theory cannot explain. It is totally illogical to maintain that they have developed the honey storage method and the organs required for it by chance. In fact, in scientific sources, we meet many realistic statements on this and similar subjects. Take, for instance, the explanation of Prof. Etienne Rabaud, Director of the Institute of Biology of the Paris University:

> These examples (for instance honey ants) show clearly that various organs have not been developed for performing certain functions by the living beings, although their prior existence has sometimes led to certain acts and tasks to be performed and sometimes not. This shows that the organs have not developed out of the adaptation by living beings to life conditions, but life conditions have arisen out of prior existence of such organs and out of their functions as we have seen. The following question may be asked as Darwin did: Does the event of clearing, or weeding out of one who loses the capacity to live, or the adaptation of organs to new conditions take place in this evolution? We contend that events have proven that such an evolution, or such a change, has not occurred. In fact, a totally different phenomenon has taken place.[31]

These explanations given by Professor Rabaud show us clearly a conclusion that anyone may arrive at by thinking with his conscience for just a very short time. A sole Creator Who is the real source of knowledge and intellect has created all living beings with their faultless organs and perfect behaviour. This truth has been expressed in the Qur'an as follows:

He is Allah, the Creator, the Maker, the Giver of Forms. To Him be-

long the Most Beautiful Names: Everything in the heavens and earth glorifies Him. He is the Almighty, the All-Wise. (Surat Al-Hashr: 24)

Wood Ants

Wood ants are famous for the hills they build from pine needles and thin branches on top of their underground nests. The nest is usually founded around a tree log. The portion of the nest above ground, made up of twigs, leaf stems, and pine needles, is the roof of the nest. This roof may reach up to 2 metres in height, it prevents seepage of rain inside and regulates the temperature of the nest in very hot or very cold weather.[32]

Wood ants, like the others, are also very hard working. They keep redecorating their nests continuously. They transfer the original surface layer to the lower layers in stages and they bring up material from the lower layers to replace the upper level. An interesting observation was made of the changes the ants make in the nest. Blue dye was sprayed on top of the hill of the nest and in four days it was observed that the top of the hill was again brown. Blue particles were found 8-10 cms below the surface. Within one month these particles went down to a depth of 40 cm. Subsequently, these blue particles have reached the surface once again.

Well, do these ants perform this continuous transportation process just for the sake of doing it? No. Researchers explain why wood ants engage in this perpetual act as follows: The perpetual motion dries the humid substances inside at the surface and prevents the formation of fungi. Otherwise, the ants would have a nest occupied by harmful fungi.

In such a situation there are two possibilities. One is that very long ago the ants, by their own research, discovered the fact that fungi develop in a humid environment, (something which man discovered as a result of long term scientific research) and developed the most rational method to eliminate this problem! The other possibility is that the conception and implementation of this perfect process can only be through inspiration by a supreme intellect. The impossibility of the first case is obvious. The One Who has inspired the ants to protect themselves from the fungi and shown them how to do so is, of course, the Almighty Allah.

In the picture, a wood ant nest is shown. The height of these nests built by wood ants from pine needles and twigs may reach approximately 2 metres.

Different Reproduction Methods of Wood Ants

The males and queens of wood ants are winged. However, they do not fly by a nuptial flight as other small ant species do. Mating is realized on the surface of the nest or some place nearby. After mating, the queen picks off its wings and does one of the following three things:

(1) She returns to the nest where she has previously lived as a larva and leaves her eggs there.

(2) Sometimes she leaves the nest with workers carrying her and looks for a new place to build a nest.

(3) If she leaves on her own, she enters the nest of smaller related species, like the black ant Formica Fusca, and replaces the queen there. The queen leaves her eggs to be looked after by the Fusca workers in there. For a while there are both guest workers and host workers in the nest. However, since the hosts do not have a queen, after a while the workers die and the wood queens acquire an established nest without doing anything.[33]

Wood ants are very well armed for war. When faced with danger, the wood ant bends the lower part of its abdomen from between its legs and squirts formic acid on its enemy. Or, during fighting, it bites the enemy with its pointed chin and injects acid in the wound. With these features, the animal acts like a chemical weapon.
Its producing formic acid in its body without giving any harm to itself and its managing to use it in the best way are, no doubt, indications of a flawless design.

In the tactics of queen wood ants discussed in section 3, a clear consciousness is observed. However, it is obvious that such consciousness may not belong to the ant itself. The queen ant has never seen any place other than the few square metres within her nest. She goes inside a colony which she has never seen or has not known of before, and knows who she should eliminate in that colony. She achieves this by overcoming all obstacles. All these factors prove beyond doubt that the queen ant is acting under inspiration. The above mentioned phenomena are clear proof of the power and sovereignty of Allah over all living creatures.

Legionary Ants

One of the most feared animals of the forests is the legionary ant. The reason for the name "army" being given to this ant community is their acting under a true military discipline.

Legionary ants are carnivores and they eat up everything in sight. Each ant is 6 to 12 millimetres long, but their incredible number and discipline make up for the disadvantage of their small size.

Direct sunlight may kill the legionary ants in a short time. Therefore they travel either at night or in the shade. Due to their sensitivity to light, they dig long tunnels while advancing. Most of the ants run in these tunnels without going outside. This does not decrease their speed, because they can dig the tunnels very fast with their strong jaws. Thus, running is both fast and secret. Legionaries move as very large armies, going over all obstructions except fire and water, although they are totally blind.[34]

Legionary ants tear their prey apart where they find it and carry small pieces of it to their temporary nests. Quite a lot of food is needed for a legionary ant colony. The approximate daily need of a medium size colony, consisting of 80,000 adult ants and 30,000 larvae, is about half a gallon (2.27 litres) of animal

Legionary ants who have formed a temporary nest by hanging on to each other with their feet.

product food.[35]

Since legionary ants do not have a fixed nest, they are always moving. The movements and migrations of the colonies depend on the production cycle. The queen produces approximately 25-35,000 eggs during two days each month. A few days before the laying of the eggs, the colony halts and gathers in a wide area. The ants hang on to each other by their hook shaped legs and form a temporary nest. The empty space in the middle acts as a chamber ready for the queen and the new generation. Here, naturally, the legs and joints of the ants at the very top are subject to excessive loading. Yet, since they are built to endure weights several hundred times more than their own weights, they can hold the whole colony without much problem.[36]

To hunt most efficiently, the ants time their movements to the needs of a developing brood, alternating between sedentary and nomadic phases. During the resting period of about 20 days, the fat, immobile queen produces 50,000 to 100,000 eggs while other offspring lie in the quiescent pupal stage. On most days, workers, foraging only for themselves and the queen, make short raids from the nest in a rosette pattern. On each raid they vary their direction by an average of 123 degrees, thus avoiding recombing the same ground.[37]

Ants can unerringly calculate the 123° by themselves, something which man cannot calculate without an instrument. This would appear to indicate a thorough knowledge of mathematics. Yet ants do not know math, they cannot even count. So this shows that what they do is done by special inspiration, and not consciously.

When the first larvae hatch, workers collect food and, in the meantime, the community stays stationary. Pieces of food are fed directly to the larvae. The queen's being ready for laying again usually coincides with earlier larvae's transition into the pupa stage. In this stage, the community stops once again. The coinciding of the laying of eggs by the queen and the larvae going into the pupa stage indicates a conscious planning since it decreases the time for which the army stops.

Harun Yahya

Chained together, army ants create a living nest. On the move at all times, a colony of army ants can make no permanent home on the grounds or in trees. But each night the workers join together to create shelters out of their own bodies. First, several ants choose an object near the ground, like a log, and dangle from it with their claws interlocked. Other ants arrive, run down the strands, and fasten on until strands become ropes that fuse into a mass a meter across called a bivouac; home is the entire colony of 200,000 to 750,000 individuals. At the center rests the queen and her brood. In the morning ants begin to disentangle to go out and raid.

The development of larvae prompts the older ants to start a new migration cycle. This is how it works: larvae give out a secretion when they are licked and cleaned by the workers. Research has shown that this fluid is effective in the decision to migrate.[38]

It would be a weakness of logic to claim that larvae which have not even gained the identity of an ant yet, have thought of secreting such a fluid and have directed the whole colony towards fulfilling their needs. The only thing that a smart observer can spot is the existence of a supreme Creator and His information and sovereignty that are all around us.

Velvet Ants

Velvet ants, which lead their lives in deserts, have excessively hairy bodies. Their natural coat serves as a heat-isolating layer. It preserves the heat in during the cold nights of the desert, and protects them from the heat during the day. Male velvet ants, because of their wings, are able to avoid the heat of the sand by flying. Yet female velvet ants have to walk around on hot sand, because they have no wings. They need this coat to be protected from the heat coming from ground as well as from the sun.

Then, what is the explanation for the insect having such a "coat" to protect it from adverse weather conditions? It is impossible to claim that the animal has acquired it by adapting to nature as part of the process of evolution, because this would lead to many questions remaining unanswered: Did the female velvet ants die due to high temperatures before having such a coat? If this was the case, how did they wait for generations to have a coat "by coincidence"? Through what kind of a coincidence did they get this body?

These questions are, of course, without answers, because these insects could not have obtained their "coats" that protect them from the heat by the mechanisms evolutionists keep suggesting, because these ants cannot live without this coat, and they have no time to wait for mutations which occur very seldom - and which are all harmful. It is clear that the animals have been designed from the outset to withstand the climate they live in.

Female velvet ants look for any type of insect nest or bee hive that they can use after leaving their place of mating. When they do, they go

In these pictures two velvet ants of different species are seen. The common feature of velvet ants is their having a "coat" that would isolate them from the heat of the environment they inhabit.

inside the nest. They are equipped to fend off any eviction attempts and eventually they stay on in the nest, because the velvet ants have strong arms and a shield which allow them to go inside even bee hives. Their outer shells are exceptionally thick and hard. Zoologists claim that they have difficulty in piercing the chest of the velvet ant with a steel pin.[39]

Once inside, the velvet queen ant, which has all kinds of equipment with which to settle in the bee hives, starts feeding on the honey stock. Also, it leaves its eggs in the pupa cells of the bees or their cocoons. The ant larvae that hatch, feed on host pupae and later on they become pupae also. Bees leave the nest at the end of summer. Velvet ants spend the winter in this nest as pupae. According to one record, in a bee nest, there have been found 76 velvet ants and only two bees.[40] This example shows how effective and successful the female velvet ant is in dealing with the female bee. The queen velvet ant, using subtle tactics, captures the nest from within and gains control of the nest herself.

What can be said here is that the velvet ant knows the bees very well and, moreover, knows very well how to deceive them, too. Then can it be anybody other than the Creator of the bee Who inspires her with the physical characteristics of the bee, its life style and nest structure? The only logical explanation is the acceptance of the existence of a sole Creator Who has created ants, bees and, in fact, all living beings.

Fire Ants

Fire ants are red insects of diminutive size. Yet they can achieve great things in spite of their smallness. The queens of these ants, which have 20 varieties in America alone, may produce as many as 5,000 eggs a day. While many ant species colonies have a few hundred workers, the colonies of this species have about half a million workers. A single mated fire ant queen can produce a colony of 240,000 workers.[41]

Fire ant workers very aggressively attack their prey with poisonous needles. It has been recorded that young fire ants have injured or even killed reptiles or baby deer. Also these aggressive ants may cause power failures by tearing up electricity cables. For a while they invaded South America and caused frightening damage. The journals and magazines of that year tell us that these ants have chewed through electrical cables and caused power cuts; they have caused damage to crops worth billions of dollars; they have caused motorways to collapse and have stung people, causing allergic shocks that have rendered them helpless. They have done all this with their powerful jaws, even digging tunnels under roads causing motorways, roads to collapse and also causing other kinds of havoc in the environment.

Protection from Germs

American experts have tried various methods to prevent the above-mentioned damage done by fire ants. They considered spreading a contagious disease inside the colony by injecting germs into the flies the ants eat. Yet, astonishingly, it was seen that such flies with germs in no way hurt the ants. In the analysis it was found out that the ants have one of the most interesting defence systems in the world of living beings: a structure in their throats which protect them from germs... Because of this structure, the bacteria in anything that the ants eat were held at the throat without entering into the body.

But we have not come to the end of the protection systems of the fire ants that are the product of a superior intellect. They also spurt an anti-microbial fluid produced in their venom sacs around the nest and on the larvae. Thus, they achieve total disinfection of the nest and the larvae.[42]

These ants, equipped as they are with an extraordinary defence system, are certainly not aware of it. Can any person with a conscience claim that such a system has evolved by chance? Neither may it be claimed that the ants have founded such a system on their own. Then who is it that placed this filter in the throats of the ants, and who inspired them to produce an anti-microbial fluid? Without doubt, the Creator of such characteristics as man, ants and random luck cannot produce is Allah, Who is All-Knowing.

Hard Working Ants

The defense specialist fire ants are also highly skilled and hard working. They may build hills 30 cm high and 60 cm wide, or they can dig labyrinthine tunnels that can go 1.5 m deep under ground. In certain areas, fire ants have built small hills numbering up to 350. The capacity of such small beings to set up such huge nests, of course, depends on their industriousness. Then what is the power that makes the ants one of the most industrious living beings in the world? It is truly astonishing that they work all day long without stopping or resting, and build nests dispersed over vast areas. Not a single one says, "I worked too hard today, let me rest a bit," or "I don't want to work today. Let me sit in a corner." This is a subject that must be carefully considered. It must not be forgotten that there are times when human beings give in to exhaustion, even when they know they have to conclude a task, and there are times when they do not apply their will, because they are tired or they feel lazy. Yet ants display great effort and the will to bring any job they start to fruition. He Who gives the ants this will and resolve, that is even stronger than that of man's, is of course the sole master of all beings – Allah.

Master Of Tactic Who Can Penetrate Defence Systems

The most frightening enemy of fire ants is Solenopsis Davgeri, which is a parasitic ant species. This living being which can penetrate their multi-leveled defence system, which even man has difficulty in understanding, is yet another ant species. It is not known how this parasite ant can "seep into" the nest of the fire ant. Yet once it is in, the parasite ant immediately attacks the queen and hangs on to her antenna, leg or throat. While the worker ants normally have to destroy any aggressor, why they do nothing against this particular creature seems hard to explain. Yet there is a simple answer. In itself attaching to her throat, the parasite imitates the pheromones of the queen. Subsequently, the workers spend all their energy in feeding this parasite that has subdued their queen, because they think that this parasite imitating her pheromones, is their queen. Their queen on the other hand dies while they think that they are feeding her.[43]

Desert Ants

It is impossible to live in burning sand at 150°F for many living beings including man. Yet there are ants who can continue to live at this temperature. Well, how can *Namib Ocymyrmex*, which is a medium-sized, long-legged, black desert ant live in such intense heat?

A typical day in the desert does not start at a certain time for Namib ants. What starts the day is the standard sand surface temperature having reached 30 degrees. Right at this point the ants start getting out of their underground nests to look for food. Since their bodies are very cold, they cannot move straight and they walk with a wobble. Yet when the temperature increases, more ants come out and they start moving straighter and faster. The temperature where the in-out traffic of the nest is highest is 52.2 degrees. When the temperature goes above this point, the movement goes on, but as it reaches 67.8 degrees, the traffic stops. This temperature is reached about one hour before noon. As the temperature starts falling in the afternoon, the food search starts again and continues until the surface temperature drops to 30 degrees.

These ants may look for food for about six days away from the nest without becoming a prey to any animals. During this time they carry food home weighing 15-20 times their own weight.

Ants, who find it impossible to return to the nest when the temperature in the desert becomes impossibly high, use quite an interesting method for protection from heat. The air temperature decreases as one rises above the sand. For instance, while the temperature of the sand is 67.8 degrees, a little above it, the air temperature is 55 degrees. Therefore, when the sand surface temperature is above 52.2 degrees, ants climb on to objects like plants and stay there for a while to cool. The temperature of the small body of the ant soon falls to the ambient temperature. In tree trunks, the temperature varies between 30 and 38.3 degrees. These cooling breaks make it possible for the ant to look for food in burning heat, albeit intermittently.

In high temperatures, if the ant cannot find a cool place within a few seconds, it is going to die from heat. In fact, in sand temperatures of over 52.2 degrees, they take such a risk every time they leave their nests. Then how have desert ants escaped this inevitable end? Since they do not measure the temperature with a thermometre, we can safely say that they came into existence knowing what to do at what temperature – and knowing these things from the very first time they left the nest.

Yes, the desert ant has been created and equipped with special features to live in the desert. Allah, Who has created a sharp jaw for leaf cutter ants has inspired in the desert ants the knowledge of how to protect themselves.

SYMBIOSIS

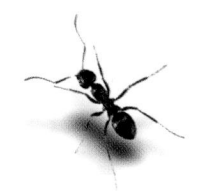

There is a basic logic to be used in analyzing evidence of the creation of living beings. We can explain this logic with a simple example.

While walking on barren land, you suddenly find a metal key on the ground. Imagine that you pick up this key without knowing what it's good for and you keep on walking. Again imagine that you come up to an empty house a few hundred metres from where you found the key. And again imagine that you try the key in the lock of the house, thinking it might work.

If the key opens the door of this house easily, what conclusion do you arrive at logically?

It is simple. You conclude that this key belongs to the door of this house. That is, it has been designed specially to open this lock. It is obvious that the same craftsman has manufactured both the lock and the key. Therefore the harmony between them is the product of a conscious design.

Yet, if somebody says to you, "You're wrong. The key you found bears no relation to that lock. It is pure coincidence that that key fits that lock, what do you think?" Of course, you will find this proposition deficient in logic, because in this world there are millions of locks and millions of keys that do not fit. It is obviously impossible for two that fit perfectly, out of millions of different ones, to be located beside each other coincidentially.

Especially if the said key is quite complex with all kinds of ins and outs, that is if it is not straight and simple like a room key. The claim of "coincidence" becomes even more absurd because, each detail on the key must have its counterpart in the lock as well, thus decreasing the probability of this coincidence millions of times.

If there are three locks to the door and you have found not one but three keys lying beside each other and all three keys have each opened one of the locks, would you believe an allegation that these keys are pieces of metal that fit the locks by chance? Furthermore, would you not think that the person who makes such a claim either has mental problems or is trying to deceive you and hide something from you?

The logical result presented by this example is simple but very significant: If there is a one-to-one fit between two independent pieces, that is, all details of these two pieces are in perfect harmony, this proves that there is a deliberate design somewhere. The key fits the lock because it has been consciously made by a skilled craftsman. A video cassette goes into a video machine easily and sits in it perfectly because it has been designed by a purposeful designer.

Looking at all these, the following general solution may be arrived at. If there is harmony between two living beings which is realized by the perfect fit of different organs, we can say that this harmony is clear proof of conscious creation. Since the existing harmony indicates a consciousness that may not be explained by chance and since the source of this consciousness may not be these animals, it is inevitable that we accept the existence of a conscious Creator Who "designs" these animals.

Now, we can re-enter the world of the ants by using this fundamental logic. Our subject in this chapter is certain living beings, who live together and show striking harmony with the ants.

Animals Who Live Together With the Ants

It has been known for over a century that many species of insects exist which live together with the ants and that there are symbiotic relations between them. Many of these do this as ransackers. The others live as dependants for part or all of their lives in the ant colony. These parasitic visitors of ants include various insects, such as sacred beetles, ticks, flies and wasps.

Some of these may live in the ant nests and benefit from all social rights. In certain cases, the ants tolerate them, although they eat the larvae and eggs of their hosts. They are not only admitted into the nest, but their larvae are fed and raised as if they were the hosts'.

Well, why do the ants allow such aggression and how is it that these insects can stay in the nest of an ant which has had a superior defence system for years? Let us analyze the phases of this inexplicable phenomenon.

As you know, there is a complex communication system within the ant colony. Because of this system, the ants may distinguish members of their colonies from strangers. This distinguishing ability serves as "a social defence system". However, the visitors we mention above manage to get into the ant nests by various techniques. This shows that they have somehow solved the communication and distinguishing ciphers of the ants. In other words, they have the ability to talk ant language by mechanical and chemical methods.

Imitation

There is a typical movement that an ant makes when it meets another ant. It touches the other ant lightly with its antenna and checks its pheromones. Then, both ants go on their way. It is known that they do this to recognize each other and to protect themselves from alien creatures.

Worker ants do the same thing when they meet insects living in their nests. Sometimes they realize that the other creature is someone different and throw it out of the nest. Yet sometimes they treat the other insect as if it were an ant. This acceptance takes place due to chemical imitation by the said insects.

It has been conclusively accepted that insects achieve this imitation totally by chemicals, because ants have thrown out insects very similar to them physically when they found them different chemically. Yet certain parasites that have no resemblance to ants at all have been accepted as if they were members of the ant nest.[44] It is very difficult to explain how such insect species learn to imitate the chemical characteristics of the ants. Such a thing can only be explained by these pheromones being added to these insects by design. An insect could not solve a chemical reaction, even if it lived for millions of years. Therefore, it must have acquired such characteristics by the conscious design of the Creator.

Hydrocarbon-Producing Insect and Fire Ants

Scarabaeid, which is an insect species, and fire ants are able to live together, because the hydrocarbons they bear are the same. If we think about insects being enemies of the ants, it is quite astonishing that a harmonious relationship exists between these two living beings. Then how can this agreement be explained?

These bugs also have the hydrocarbons that ants have and they also have other hydrocarbon series with a high molecular weight. When insects leave the nests of the ants, the compounds which they have in common with the ants disappear, but the heavy hydrocarbons belonging to them remain. Later, when they go to the colony of another fire ant species, this time they produce the scent of this colony.[45]

When the bug first arrives at the nest of the fire ants, it depends on its own thick shell and tries to protect itself by pretending that it is dead. In a few days, after simulating the hydrocarbon of the ants, it is fully admitted into the ant nest.[46]

How can an insect of this species imitate any scent and secrete it in its own body? How does it know that by producing this scent it will be able to fool the ants into admitting it to their nest? Can a bug achieve all this on its own?

Of course not. Getting to know the ants by their chemical and physical characteristics is just not something that a bug can do on its own. It would be quite absurd to say that these bugs have gone through evolution by living with the ants for a long time and eventually developed the ability to produce the scent of the ants chemically. No mutation or coincidence can lead to the development of such a complex characteristic. The only possible conclusion is the existence of a Creator, Who has given powers of recognition and imitation to this bug. The One Who makes it possible for ants and bugs to exist in harmony together and Who prevents their acting in a hostile manner towards each other, is Allah, the Creator of the two animal species.

Visitors of Army Ants

There are ticks that live on the bodies of army ants. These tick species feed on the blood they get from the membrane-like area at the back of the ant they live on, or the fatty secretions on the bodies of their hosts. Sometimes these ticks live on the tip of the rear leg of the ant and, at times, they allow their whole bodies to be used as part of the ant's foot by proxy.

As explained before, army ants form chains by hanging on to each other by their legs when they form temporary nests out of these chains. In the laboratory analyses made, it has been observed that in the ants that hold on to another worker with the tick on their legs, the rear legs of the tick took the form of the ant's claws and performed the same function. These ticks, with their clutching mechanisms in the form of teeth on their backs, have been equipped with appropriate back formations so that they may adapt to the body of the ant.[47]

It is impossible that these two creatures who are complementary to each other, have found each other among thousands of species living in nature only by a lucky chance. The probability of these two species – which depend on each other for survival – having met one day, having seen that their bodies were suitable for co-existence and having decided on symbiosis is zero. Therefore, this perfect harmony is likewise just another one of the details showing perfect creation by Allah. Yet these small details are too valuable to pass by. These examples, of which we may witness thousands or millions every day, have been created so that man may see the infinite power, the knowledge and the fine art of Allah.

Smart Fly Larva

The bodies of the ants form a very suitable location for parasitic beings. Therefore many species of parasites choose as their homes the bodies of ants. What is worth mentioning is *Strongygaster globula*, which is a type of fly.

The larva of this fly ("Endo parasite" or Interior parasite) lives in the rear section of the body of the queen that forms the ant colony. The behaviour of the queen in this situation is not affected noticeably apart from its stopping laying eggs. When the larva of the parasite leaves the body of the host, it goes into the pupa phase and is treated by the ants as if it is one of their own pupa. Yet, during the flying phase, this friendly attitude is abandoned and the fly is forced to leave the nest and the queen ant dies after the parasites have left the nest.[48]

The settling of fly larvae on the body of the ant, and living on it, is truly an exceptional situation. It is impossible for a newly born creature to have chosen the body of a queen ant as a home for itself. The choosing by the mother fly of such a location to lay her eggs can be possible only if she has a prior and thorough knowledge of the body and life style of the ant. Because in its own habitat, there are hundreds of different living species that it may leave its eggs on. The fly, which is attentive towards its babies, identifies the most suitable one and for its home, selects the queen ant. However, it is impossible for her to anticipate that her eggs will grow here under protection and that the ants will in fact take care of them. Because a fly is a totally different creature from an ant and it is impossible for it to know anything about the ant.

Then we can say that this correct decision made by the fly is not the result of "foreseeing the future" by this small animal, but a program within it, in other words, a given inspiration. The One Who places the larva in the most appropriate living area is Allah, Who is totally sovereign over the fly and the ant and has infinite knowledge of them, because He is the Creator, Owner and Sovereign of all living beings.

In these pictures, six different parasite species that live on the army ants are seen. These parasites have settled on the ants in different symbiotic adaptations. (1) The parasite on the top feeds on the body fluids of the ant on which it inhabits. (2) The second parasite is a type of mite and lives on the tip of the foot of its host. (3) This interesting parasite species deceives the ants and feeds on their larvae. (4) This species spends most of its time on the worker ants. (5) It has chosen the tip of the ant's chin as its home. (6) This parasite species has settled in the antenna root of the ant.

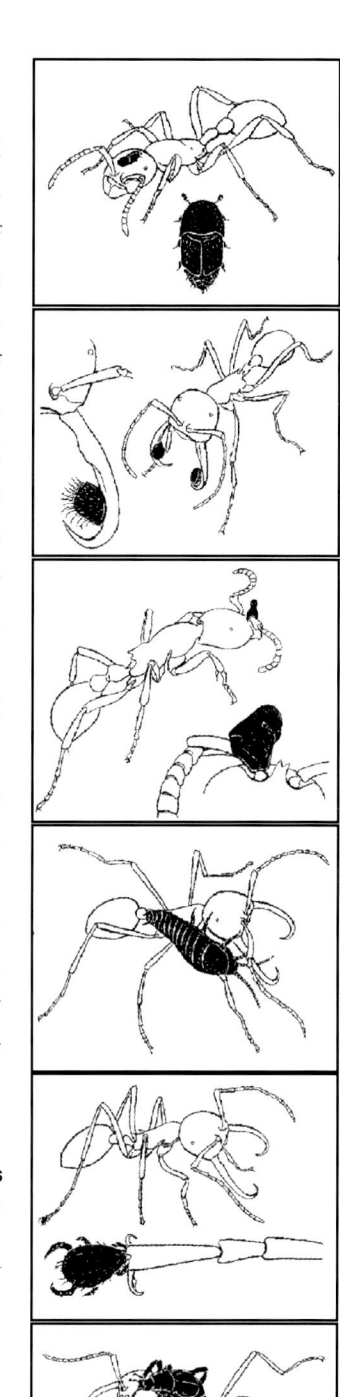

Secret of Blue Butterflies

In 1979, the large blue butterfly died out from its last breeding sites in England. Researchers who studied were not able to find out for a long time why the butterfly disappeared as there seemed to be plenty of the right habitat (rough grassland), with lots of the wild thyme plants on which the butterfly lays its eggs. Actually, the secret was hidden in the amazing life cycle of the butterfly.

After the caterpillars hatch, they feed on thyme for about three weeks. Then they drop to the ground and give out a liquid that is attractive to red ants. When a red ant appears, the caterpillar rears up and swells the skin behind its head, tricking the ant into thinking it is one of its own grubs. The ant carries the caterpillar back to its nest, and it lives in the nest for almost a year, feeding on the ant grubs and spending the winter in hibernation. In spring, it makes a silk cocoon. While inside the cocoon, it slowly changes into an adult butterfly, before finally leaving the nest in midsummer.

The discovery of this parasitism has eliminated the shroud of secrecy over the extinction of the butterfly species. Due to an ecological change in the region, the red ants had moved away and the caterpillars that hatched there were killed by other ant species, which were not fooled by them.[49]

Now, the questions to be answered are the following: Could this co-existence have been formed by luck? How does the butterfly – as a caterpillar, which is not even an adult butterfly yet – know how to fool an ant? How have the organs come into being which make it possible for it to look like an ant when inflating its back? Since evolutionists do not accept conscious creation, they would argue that these organs have emerged by coincidence. Yet no coincidence can result in such a perfect likeness. It is impossible for this similarity to have formed in time in stages, because a caterpillar which has not yet acquired this likeness would be hunted down by the ants and would not be able to survive. Since it is impossible for the caterpillar to give shape to itself consciously, the only answer is that this animal was given its shape and made to resemble the ant by a Creating Will, that is, Allah.

In the picture on the left we see the large blue butterfly after leaving the ant nest. The picture on the right shows the blue butterfly caterpillar before meeting the ants.

In the picture (above right), the imitating caterpillar is taken by the ant to its own nest. The picture on the left shows the blue butterfly caterpillar living among the larvae in the ant nest.

Parasites that are Fed from the Mouth of the Ant

A type of parasite called *Dinarda*, tours around the nest of the colony and feeds upon the prey brought in by the host ants. Also, it utilizes the nutritional fluids of the host. This parasite wanders around the nest chambers where the newly arrived workers and hunters share food. Its tactic is to touch the edge of its mouth when it sees the ant so that it will give it a drop of food. Actually, by this feeding method, it places itself in enormous danger, because once the ant realizes that the parasite is a stranger, it is going to assume the attack position. Yet the parasite has taken its precautions against such circumstances. When it sees that the ant is getting ready to attack, it raises its belly upwards and spurts a tranquilizing fluid towards the ant. The attack ends because of this fluid and the parasite escapes.[50]

Smart Immigrants

Some insect species *(Atemeles)* leave the ant nest *(Formica)* where they have been raised during the summer, and migrate to the nest of another ant species *(Myrmica)*. After wintering over there, they come back to their original nest in summer. There is of course a reason for these moves: There is no growing period in Formica nests in winter months. Therefore, the food flow decreases. Yet, in the Myrmica species, there is a brooding period and food sources are very rich.[51]

It might be expected that during this migration, the migrants would have difficulty in finding their way back. However, they have absolutely no difficulty. The Formica nests are in wooded areas and the Myrmica nests are in green, grassy areas. The immigrants who leave the Formica nest have discovered a very important method of finding their way: they go towards the light and find the grassy land that is the location of the nest they will settle in. Yet when they arrive there, another problem awaits them. They have to differentiate between Myrmica ants and other ant colonies. Research shows that the migrants spot the correct host because of the scent given out of the Myrmica nest.[52] In short, these immigrants have the capacity to distinguish between the scents of ant colonies, apart from their skill in finding their direction by the aid of light.

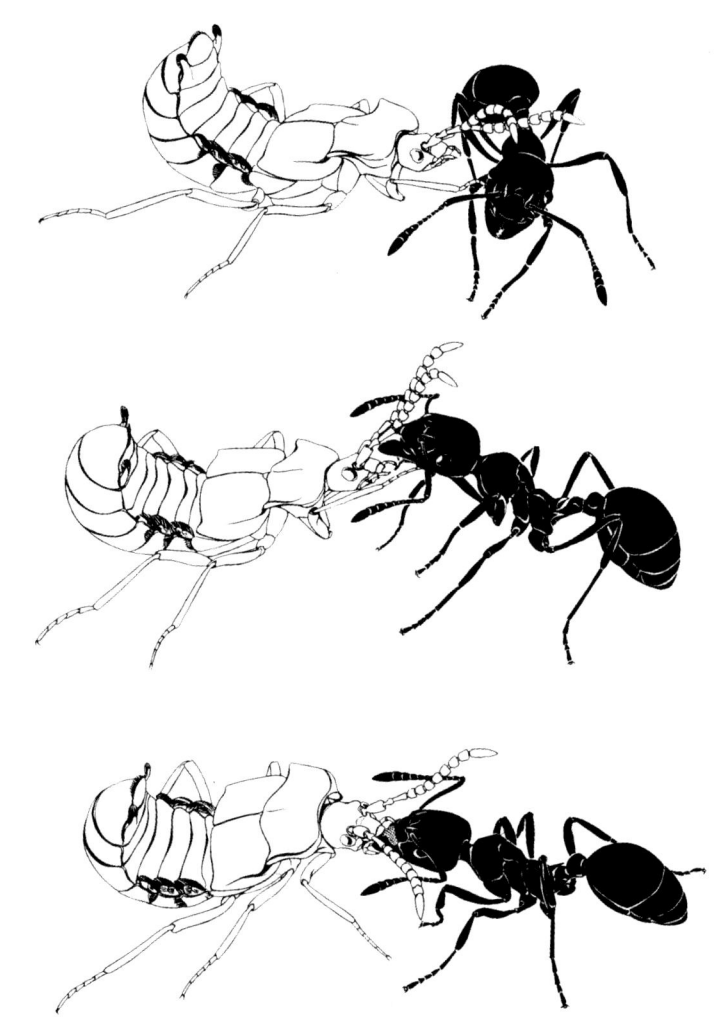

In the picture on the left, we see the food exchange between a bug and an ant. Above, the bug touches the ant with its antennae. In the middle, the bud taps the ant's mouth with its forelegs. At the bottom, the ant presents a drop of liquid food to the imitating bug.

These migrants who change nests twice a year are very interesting, because they are accepted by both ant species and are able to adapt to the nest environment immediately. Wasmann, who has been doing research on ants for many years, believes that this species is the most advanced cohabitant with its still unsolved adaptation method. They have a very astonishing feature that they use in getting themselves admitted to the nest they are migrating to. These migrants have a gland that produces defensive substances and they use a potent chemical secretion they produce there to pacify their enemies when attacked. This chemical is so strong that it was observed that the ants treated the parasite a lot more "gently" when they spurted this secretion on to the ants in whose homes they had been living for a long time.[53]

Such conscious activities of migrant bugs set one to thinking. As this bug knows when to move to which nest, it must know ants in every way. Then how has this migration adventure started? First of all, it must choose among many species of insects and decide to cohabit in an ant nest. After making this tough selection among hundreds of species of insects, it must pick the one most suitable for it among 8800 ant species and then realize that the food supply of the selected ants is decreasing during winter. Then after noticing this, it must discover the nest where

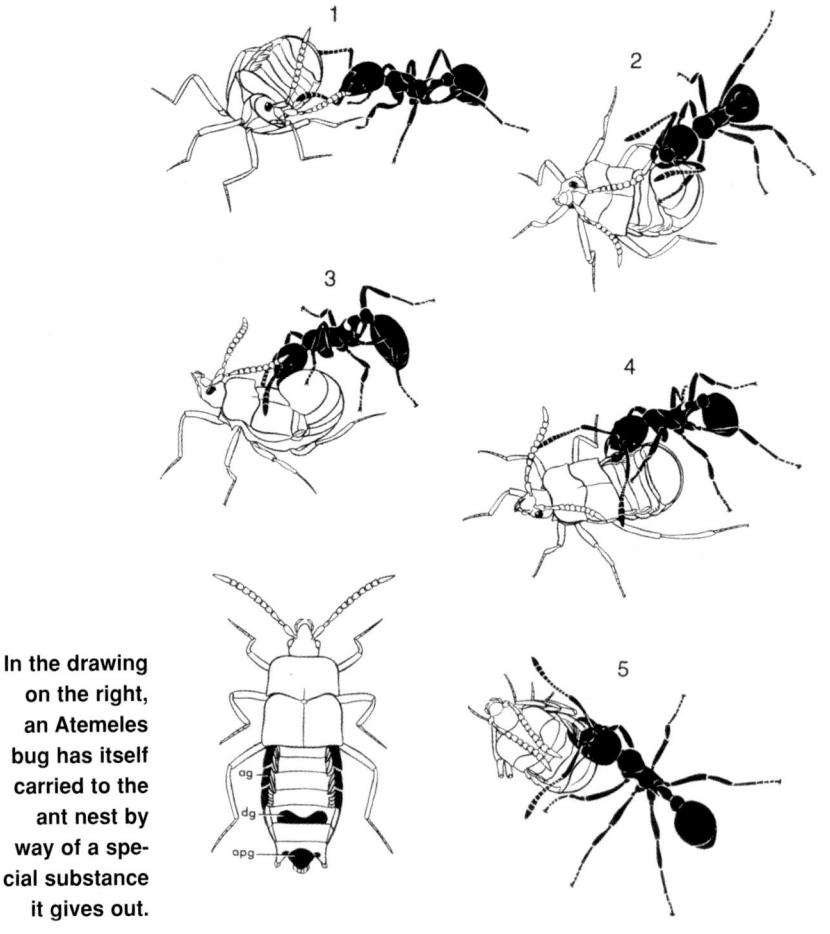

In the drawing on the right, an Atemeles bug has itself carried to the ant nest by way of a special substance it gives out.

food is abundant in winter. The creature who has to make all these decisions is an insect such as we will probably never come across in our entire lives. It is quite illogical to expect an insect to make such decisions.

Still, even if we believe that this system has developed in such a way, the questions we face do not come to an end. How does this insect arrive at the nest while moving from one nest to the other? When it's very difficult to find the way in the forest even for an intelligent person, how can a migrant insect which is one thousandth the size of a man contrive to find an ant hill in a huge forest?

The answer, "by going towards the light" does not really provide any explanation, because light may be coming from at least 2-3 different fronts. There are areas many square metres wide, where it arrives by going towards the light, before the nest it seeks may be found. (Let us not forget that for a creature the size of an insect, an area measured in square metres is the same as several square kilometres for us). Here, the scent recognition process starts, but that too is quite astonishing, because it is very difficult to distinguish a single scent from all the others in a forest where hundreds of ant colonies live and where also thousands of different scents other than those of the ants exist. Moreover, it is interesting that an insect, which spends a whole summer somewhere else, can keep this scent in its memory.

Lastly, let us think about the following: even if we pick up this insect and put it in front of the entry to the suitable ant nest ourselves, it will be very difficult for it to live in it because, as we know, ants also have very strong recognition ability. As they do not accept even an ant which does not belong to their colony, they will of course treat this insect as hostile and will throw it out of the nest. However, things do not turn out like this and the insect is treated quite hospitably. It is argued that this is because of the positive effect of a chemical which it gives out from its body. Then how does the migrant insect know that it can influence the ants with this substance and understand that it can reverse this hostile behaviour? Has it succeeded in producing the ideal substance by deciding to manufacture it itself?

Of course, it is impossible to answer these questions positively. There is an obvious picture that one can see. The said insect is doing things which require serious intelligence and a sense of judgement. Yet, it would be absurd to think of the ability to think and to judge in such a creature as does not even have a brain. We have to admit that the source of intelligence in the things the insect does is another power "outside" the animal.

Evolutionists have produced the phrase intuition to overcome this dead end that they are facing, and they have argued that animal behaviour is the result of certain motives of unknown source. Yet this phrase is just whitewashing and does not change anything. The picture is still clear: There are motives which dominate the animal that are the result of an intelligent programming. Since there is no intelligent programming by the animal itself, the source of such motives must be another power ruling the animal. This power belongs to Him Who is not seen, but rules over the visible world with supreme wisdom and reflects such knowledge in living beings, like insects, which are themselves not endowed with consciousness.

Insect that Imitates the Dead

Ant nests provide a food source, a shelter from aggressors and appropriate living conditions for an insect species that live in the southern deserts of the USA and Mexico. Once these insects manage to penetrate an ant nest, they automatically go to a brooding room and feed on ant larvae.

These have developed various techniques to get inside an ant nest. Some species walk directly towards the entrance of the ant nest, then go through the heaps of plant stems into the nest. These bugs have shells that protect them very well. Therefore the ants cannot kill them. They can only attack in unison and throw them out.

Unsuccessful bugs never give up. This time they imitate the dead and seem attractive to the ants, so the ants take them home as food. To fool the ants, these bugs expertly imitate the dead by pulling their antennae back and stiffening their legs.[54]

Once they reach the egg chambers, the ants for some reason give up on these insects. Research has shown that while these bugs are feeding on ant eggs, the fluid given out by their hair attracts the attention of the ants elsewhere. Thus, the aggression of the ants is decreased and they are not able to protect their eggs.[55]

Also these "intelligent" bugs leave their own larvae in the ant nest. Bug larvae grow up here among piles of shredded vegetation. Although they have no defence mechanism against ants, they are not attacked by ants and, in time, they become able to defend themselves against the ants and to escape through skilled manoeuvring.[56]

Fly Larvae That Know Ants

We are going to see a striking and perfect example of creation below: the fly larvae that can do imitations.

The larvae of syrphid flies *(Microdon)* overwinter deep within the ant nest and, in spring, they move to the surface of the nest to pupate. In the course of research, the larvae were observed to disappear immediately upon hatching and they were thought to be dead, with a single remaining larva clinging to the outer surface of an ant cocoon. The magnification revealed the larva becoming rounder and rounder, as if it were exerting pressure to distort its shape. Suddenly, it was simply gone. The larva had inserted its mouth hooks into the silken cocoon and created a hole large enough to allow it to enter. The disappearing larvae were simply inside the cocoons, feeding on the ant pupae and molting into the next larval stage. Microdon larvae, at later stages, folded themselves lengthwise until they were practically indistinguishable from ant cocoons. After this transformation, agitated worker ants arrived, seized the impostor young, and carried them to the safe depths of the nest.[57]

This was an unusual case of mimicry. The ants perceived the fly larvae to be ant cocoons. During research, it was noticed that the chemistry of the outer, hard cuticle of the larval flies and that of larval ants matched almost perfectly. In other words, fly larvae were able to imitate ant cocoons chemically as well.

Chemical analysis confirmed that this was a case of true chemical mimicry. Then how could the Microdon larvae employ this imitation?

On the underside of the larvae are elaborate protuberances, the function of which was not known. It is now suspected that they contain glands or glandular openings for secreting the chemicals that the larvae use to mimic their hosts.[58]

Then, how can a being who does not even know the meaning of "chemistry" perform such an impersonation? And only the larvae of Microdon flies have such a defence system, never the adults. Since this ability of impersonation is not known in adult flies, it is not something which can be thought out. This means that the larvae have this ability from birth.

No coincidence can implant a chemical order in the body of a larva that will cause it to impersonate ants. The only conclusion that may be derived from this event is that the larvae are born into this world already equipped with this feature.

Woodman Ants and Aphids

Up until now, what you have read about ants has given you a general idea about the ant world. But this is just the beginning, because there are many different species in the world of ants equipped with characteristics we do not know about. One of them is the "milkman ant" which is also known as the woodman ant.

The woodman ants in question obtain milk from leaves via aphids.

This cooperation between ants and aphids is one of the most interesting relationships in the whole world of insects.

Aphids which are placed on the leaves by ants extract the sap in the root of the plant. The plant sap that enters the body of the aphid is transformed into the substance called "nectar". The ants, which like this nectar, have found a way for aphids to give this food to them. A hungry ant approaches the aphid and starts patting it with its feelers and antennae. The aphid likes this very much and secretes a drop of nectar and gives it to the ant. In return, the ants look after their aphids very well.[59]

In the autumn, the ants pick up the aphid eggs and keep them in their nest until they hatch. Later on, they place the young aphids on the roots of various plants, so that they suck the sap and provide milk to the milkman ants.

At this point the question would be: When there are thousands of living beings in the world, how do the milkman ants know of this characteristic of the aphids? How can they select them from among all the other creatures?

It is, of course, impossible to evaluate as a chain of accidents the fluid that comes out of the aphid being exactly what the ant needs and the ant's knowing what the aphid would

"Animal Breeder" Ants. Ants, in addition to all their interesting skills, also do "animal breeding". As seen in these pictures, ants make a "flock" for themselves from aphids and use this "flock" to obtain food. In return, they look after their "flock" very well, keeping them by their side, and protecting them against their enemies. The "animal breeding" of ants is, no doubt, an interesting example of symbiosis observed in the world of insects.

like and its patting it against the food it is going to receive. Once again, there is a designed pairing, a great harmony and therefore an obvious creation.

Plants that Cohabit With Ants

The pitcher plant of Eastern India, Nepenthes Bicalcarata, allows ant colonies to inhabit in its trunk. This plant looks exactly like a pitcher and takes in and digests the insects that land on it. Yet ants are free to wander around on this carnivorous plant, picking up insects and other food material.[60]

This is to the mutual benefit of ants and this plant. The ants are under the threat of being eaten by the plant, yet they have gained a home. The plant leaves certain tissues and insect remnants to the ants and, in return, earns protection by the ants from its enemies.

This example defines the outlines of symbiosis between plants and ants. The anatomies and physiological structures of the ants and their host plant have been designed to provide this mutual relationship between them. Although defenders of evolution say that these interspecies relationships have gradually grown over millions of years, it is obvious that any claim that two such creatures as have no intelligence could agree to arrange a mutually beneficial system is untenable.

Then what is it that causes the ants to live on plants?

The tendency of the ants to live on plants is the result of a fluid secreted by the plants, called "residual nectar". This nectar fluid serves the purpose of an invitation for the ants to come to the plant. There is evidence that the plants give out this fluid at certain times. For instance, the black cherry tree actively gives out this fluid only three weeks in the year. It is certain that this timing is not coincidental, because this three-week period is the only time when the tent caterpillar assaults the black cherry and the ants can easily kill these caterpillars and protect the plant.[61]

To see how obviously this is evidence of creation, one needs nothing other than normal common sense. It is, of course, impossible to accept that the tree has calculated the period in which it is subject to the most harm and has decided that the best way to protect itself during this period would be to attract ants and that, to this end, it has produced a structural change in its own chemistry. The tree has no brain. Therefore, it can neither think, calculate, nor adjust its own chemicals. To think that this rational procedure is a characteristic acquired as a result of coincidence – which is the logic of evolution – is totally absurd. In a very obvious way, the tree is doing something which is the result of intelligence and knowledge.

Therefore, the only conclusion that may be reached here is that this feature of the tree has been formed by the will which has created the tree. It is obvious from the arrangements He has made that He is not only sovereign over the tree but also over the ants and caterpillars. If re-

Above, we see a pitcher plant which is a kind of "insect trap". Yet, this pitcher plant does not serve as a trap for certain insects. For instance, the ant shown on the next page is able to live together with the pitcher plant. The plant is disregarding the existence of the ant in an inexplicable fashion.

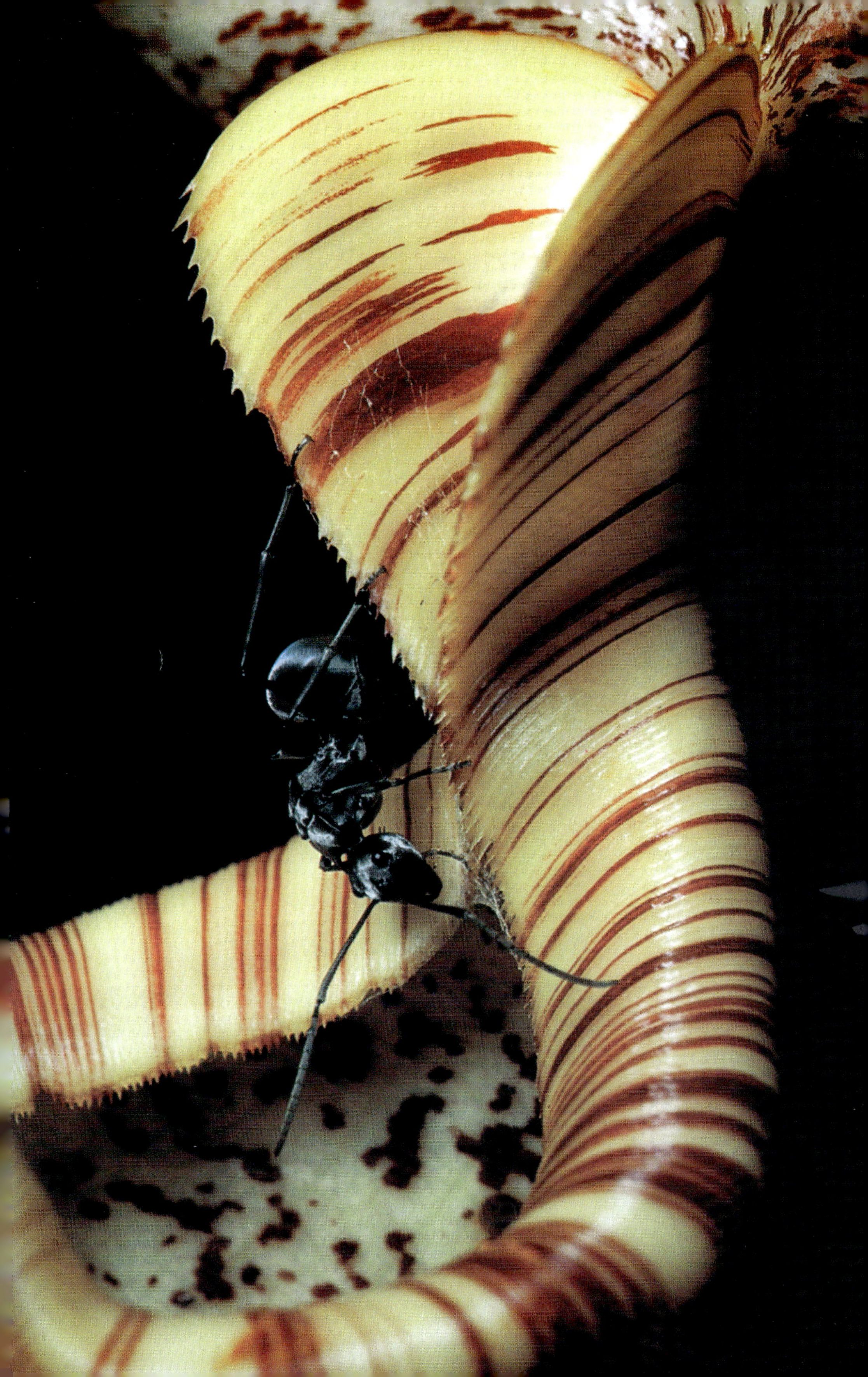

search is taken beyond this point, it is observable that, in fact, He dominates the whole of nature and has organized each component of nature separately and in harmony, thus founding the perfect system that we call "ecological balance". We can advance further and go into the domains of geology and astronomy. Everywhere we are going to face the same situation, with countless systems that function in harmony within a perfect order. These systems all indicate the existence of an organizer. Yet, none of the entities making up the systems are themselves organizers.

"Is then He Who creates like one who does not create? Will you not take heed?" (Surat an-Nahl:17)

Then that organizer must be a Will Who is aware of and sovereign over the whole universe. The Qur'an describes Him as follows:

He is Allah, the Creator, the Maker, the Giver of Forms. To Him belong the Most Beautiful Names: Everything in the heavens and earth glorifies Him. He is the Almighty, the All-Wise. (Surat Al-Hashr: 24)

The Acacia Tree and Ants

Acacia trees grow throughout the tropical and subtropical regions of the world and are protected by thorns. An ant species that lives on African acacias gnaws an entry hole in the walls of the thorns and lives permanently inside the acacia tree. Each colony of ants inhabits the thorns on one or more trees and feeds on the nectars of the acacia leaves. These colonies also eat the caterpillars and other organisms they find on the tree.

The nectar of the acacia trunk is very rich in oils and proteins. Thomas Belt, who first described these bodies, noted that their only apparent function was to nourish the ants. Ants, which live on these trees, obtain sugars from the nectaries and feed them to their larvae.[62]

What is it that the tree expects from the ants in return for its produce?

The worker ants, which swarm over the surface of the plant, are very aggressive toward other insects and, indeed, towards animals of all sizes. When their tree is brushed by an animal, they swarm out and attack at once, inflicting painfully burning bites. Moreover, other plants sprouting

The symbiosis between acacias and ants is perhaps one of the most interesting in the plant and insect worlds.

within as much as a meter of occupied acacias are chewed and mauled, and their bark is girdled. Twigs and branches of other trees that touch an occupied acacia are similarly destroyed.[63]

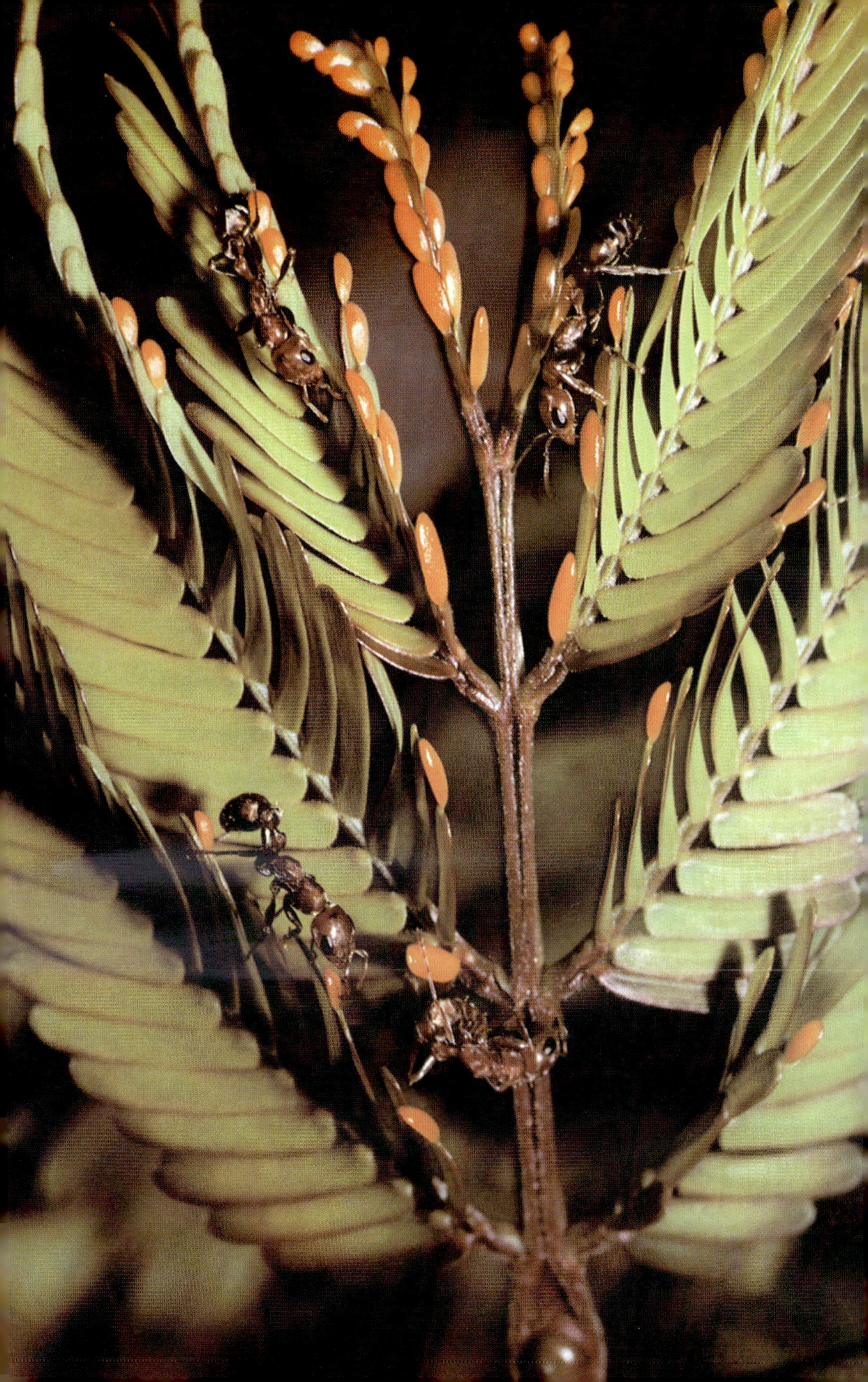

It has been shown that acacia trees which have no ants are prone to more attack and damage by other bugs compared to those which harbour ant colonies. In an experiment, it was observed that wild plants that sprang from an acacia trunk 40 centimetres in diametre were invaded by ants and chewed and trampled to destruction. Ants have even attacked the branches and leaves of other plants that touch on the shadow of the acacia. The whole ant colony is in an active state while cleaning and patrolling the plant. The conclusion researchers have arrived at is as follows: The ants are employed as a "special army" hired by the acacia.[64] Since the awareness which would promote such a negotiation is not within the capability of either side, it must be accepted that this balance must have been established by the will of Allah Who created both parties to the agreement.

Ant Hotels

In some plants, there are deep hollows called "domatia" in biological terminology. These do not serve any purpose other than that of forming a shelter for ant colonies. They have holes which allow ants to go in and out easily, or thin curtains made up of tissue. In these chambers, there

Above, an ant is seen on a plant which is an extremely suitable shelter for itself. The holes on the ant serve as "doors" for the ants.

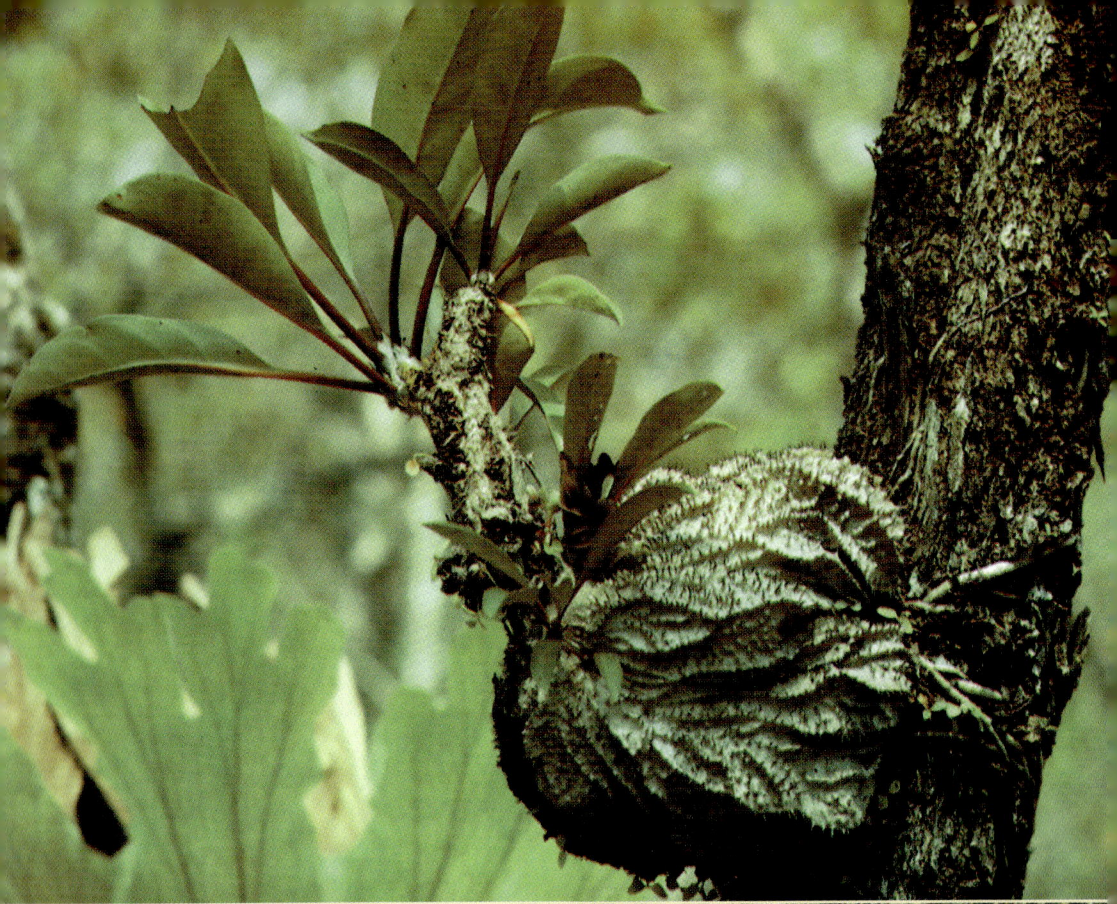
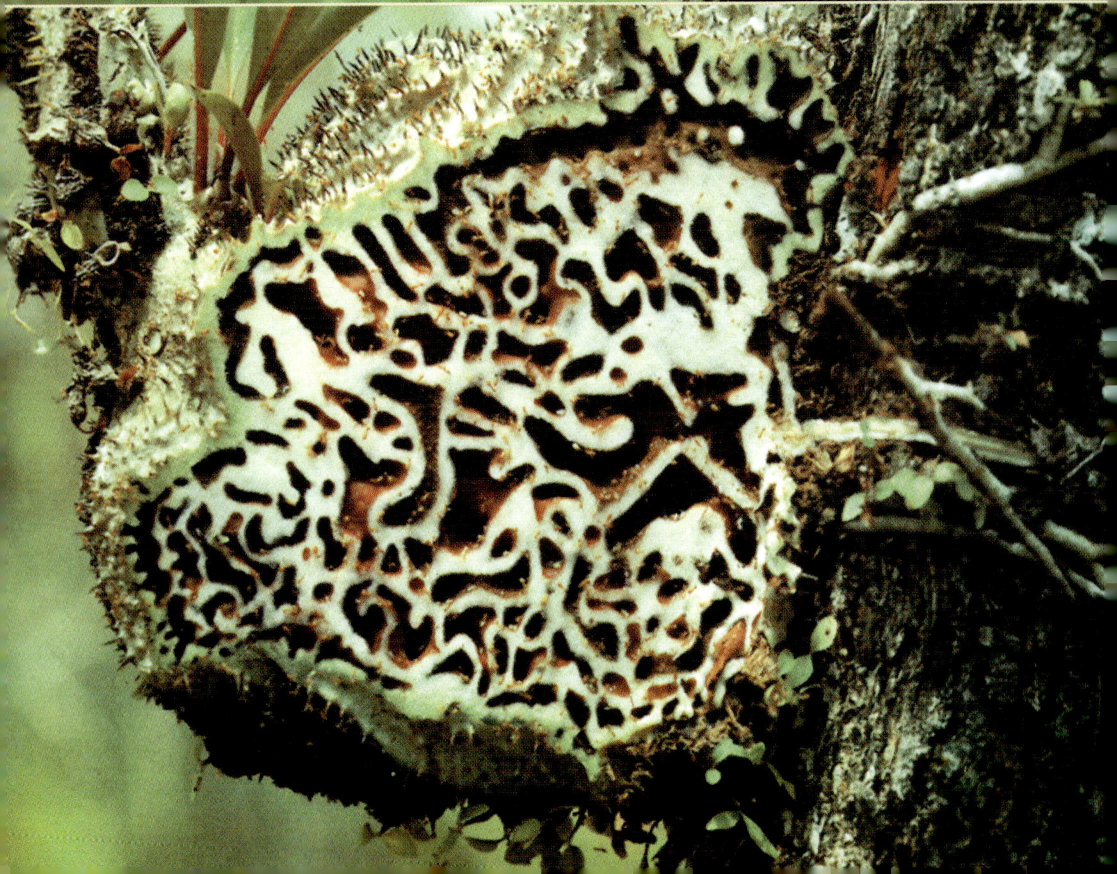

are also "forms of food" (Food the plant produces specifically for ants to be gathered and eaten). The only function of "food forms" is again just feeding the ants. They have no apparent benefit for the plant.[65]

In short, domatias are very special structures that are formed so that the ants may maintain their lives. Their temperature and humidity are ideally balanced to suit the ants' requirements. Ants live comfortably in these special places prepared just for them, almost as men do in quality hotels.

It is not possible to claim that these structures materialize by luck, that they produce food for ants by coincidence and that they take on need-based forms.

Ant-plant relationships are just one of the proofs of the incredible equilibrium created by a sole Creator on this earth. Furthermore, this relationship is mutual. The services ants provide against the services of the plants are very important factors in the plants of the world being so efficient. Ants enrich the earth in carbon by cultivating it, adding nutrition to it by their waste and excretion, and keeping the ambient temperature and humidity at an appropriate level. Therefore, plant species near ant nests are better off than those in other areas.

Ant Plant and Nitrogen Source Ant

An ant species (*Philidris*) and its host plant (*Dischidia major*) produce a very complex set of chemicals all throughout their lives.

This plant has no roots that go underground. Therefore, it winds along other plants to get support. It has a very interesting method for increasing its carbon and nitrogen gain.

Ants have a storage area in this plant where they raise their young and hide organic residues (dead ants, insect pieces, etc.) called "ant leaf". The plant uses these residues as a source of nitrogen. Also, the interior surfaces of the leaf spaces absorb the carbon dioxide given out by the ant, thus reducing dehydration from the pores.[66] Prevention of dehydration is very important for these ant plants that grow in tropical climates, because they can never reach the water in the soil, since they have no roots. Thus, ants provide for two important needs of the plant in return for its providing shelter for them.

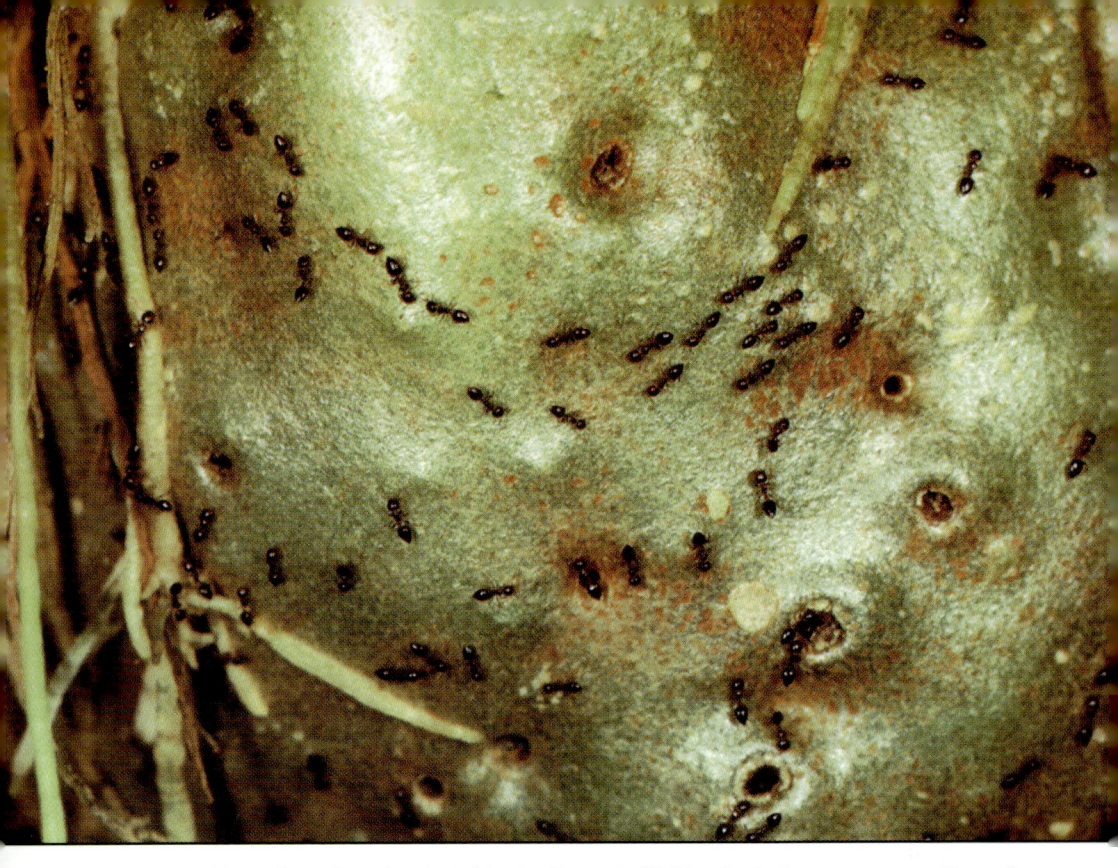

Above is a plant that is fed by its "tenants." This plant also serves as a "home" for the ants.

Ants That Feed Their Hosts

Certain ants feed their host plants. For instance, the inflated bodies of two kinds of plants (*Myrmecodia* and *Hydnophytum*) that are full of lumps provide chambers with partitions for ants to nest in them. Ants live in these grooves but, interestingly, differentiate between them. The chambers they live in have smooth walls. They pack insect remnants into the other chambers, which have rough walls. Research has shown that rough walls absorb nutritional material but that straight grooves are not porous. Therefore, the plant absorbs the insect remnants that the ants bring in. In other words, the selection the ants make as regards the use of chambers is very correct.

Scientists have carried out a very interesting test on this subject. First they fed fruit fly larvae with yeast treated with radiation. Then they placed them on the plant harbouring the ants. The ants, finding the larvae, carried them immediately to the chambers with rough textured walls. For the following two weeks, scientists tracked the level of radioactivity in the plant to prove that insect remnants were carried along the trunk after being assimilated by the plant. The scientists proved that the radioactivity was carried all over the plant, since it absorbed nutritional materials.[67]

Piper Plant and Brown Ant

The relationship between the piper plant and the ants is perhaps the most interesting of all these we have looked at so far. The ant plant called piper (treelets in the black pepper family) grows in the shade of the tropical forest of Central America. It is a plant that provides both food and shelter for brown ants (*Pheidole Bicornis*). By the time young Piper trees have just two or three full-sized leaves, one of the leaf bases - hollow swellings between the branch and the leaf itself – usually contains a Pheidole queen. The queen colonizes a Piper sapling by chewing an entrance hole and laying eggs inside the leaf base. When her eggs first hatch into larvae, she and the young occupy one of the leaf bases, but as the colony grows, the worker ants advance gradually throughout the stem pith tissue, and the entire plant becomes a domicile.[68]

This plant is also a source of food for the ants. The inside surface of the expanded leaf bases produces for them single-celled food bodies. Ants pluck these oil-and protein-rich morsels from the walls and feed them to their larvae.[69]

These rich foods that the ants will perhaps never find elsewhere, are presented to them by the piper. These ants move towards the pipers that will provide them with the best care, shelter and food each year and build their nests in the parts of the plant most suitable for them.

"Smart" Piper

The piper plant that serves as a food source has another very interesting feature. Other plant species keep on producing food even after their colonies leave, yet piper plants do this only when ants are present. Scientists have noticed that the plant stops food production in the absence of brown ants *(Pheidoles)*.[70]

Mutual Assistance

What the piper plant does is not a one-sided sacrifice because, during this mutual living process, the ant also produces nutritional material for its host.

When the ant lump in the trunk of the plant decays, it is taken inside the inner soft tissue of the plant as hydrous ammonia. This fluid is very beneficial for the plant. It increases its efficiency. As an addition, the breathing ant colony members increase the carbon dioxide concentration of the plant and ensure its being healthier.

Some research has been done to understand if piper ants provide food for their plants and it has been proven that food-seeking Pheidole ants have brought in certain particles like spores, weed pieces and moth scales. Ants keep these foods that they carry in in small sacks in which they keep larvae, and the plant takes in the required minerals from these foods.

Strategy Expert, Pheidole

Pheidole ants are quite peaceful. They move slowly. They neither attack, nor bite. Yet these ants use a shrewd strategy to protect themselves and their hosts, the piper plants.

Many insects like caterpillars that eat leaves lay their eggs on the plants. Ants remove this danger immediately. Termite eggs left on leaves of piper plants are noticed by worker ants within one hour. Then they pick them up one by one. They carry the egg to the edge of the leaf in their chin and let it drop. Researchers placed termite eggs in the larvae chambers as food for ant larvae. But the result was the same and the ants removed everything that could harm them or the plant right away.[71]

Invader Aphid

Another creature who harms the piper is the invader wheat aphid (*Ambates melanobs*). The wheat aphid attacks the majority of plants without ants and kills them by piercing the trunk of the plant through to the inside. But these micro invaders cannot be very successful if the plant has ant guards. Ants attack the defenceless soft built wheat aphid larvae as soon as they start tunnelling into the inner part of the trunk.

Strategist ants who defend the plant, they live on against all kinds of invasions and also protect the ecological balance with this feature of theirs.

The plant and ants co-existing in such harmony cannot be explained by coincidences. The picture we build up from the information given right throughout this entire chapter shows us species that are different from each other but who have been created for full cooperation.

At the beginning of this chapter, we have given a similar example of such harmony: The relationship between a key and the lock it opened. There was a single explanation for the harmony between these two separate objects. The lock and the key were both made by the same master, that is, they were consciously designed. In the examples of cooperation we meet in nature, the same logic applies. The ant and the plant cooperate because they are the products of conscious design. Neither is the ant dominant over the plant, nor is the reverse true. Incapable of forming ideas, they are both simply acting under the inspiration of their Creator, and thus are able to maintain a reciprocity that allows them to pursue their lives on earth.

The task for people, then, is to see this conscious creation and recognize its owner. Yet, many do not think about this, nor do they care. The following verses state in the best way possible this perfect creation by Allah and the blindness of people towards it:

> **Mankind! An example has been made, so listen to it carefully. Those whom you call besides Allah are not even able to create a single fly, even if they were to join together to do it. And if a fly steals something from them, they cannot get it back. How feeble are both the seeker and the sought! They do not measure Allah with His true measure. Allah is All-Strong, Almighty. (Surat al-Hajj: 73-74)**

DEFENCE AND WAR TACTICS

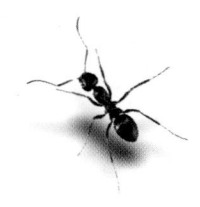

In the previous chapters we have seen that the social order of ants is highly advanced. These hardworking, productive and sacrificing beings have yet another feature: They defend themselves very successfully against enemies and they use very interesting techniques to fight for the survival of the colony.

The small size of the ant at first gives the impression that they are defenceless. One cannot even imagine that these creatures, which can be crushed easily by stepping on them, can achieve tasks that seem far beyond their capacities. Yet, Allah within the unique ecological order He has created on earth has designated their place and has equipped them with the necessary defence mechanisms.

By Allah's inspiration ants use seemingly incredible tactics and strategies to defend their colonies and to protect themselves against the enemies that they meet during the search for food. While developing hunting strategies, they fight not to become a prey to others. One battle of this type is the one between the ant colonies.

War Between Colonies

One of the most important reasons for inter-colonial wars is the difficulty in sharing food resources. In such wars, the ant species that first finds the food source usually wins. This is because the discovering ants surround the food, thus preventing others from getting at pieces of the food. They also leave their scents around, so that members of the following colony cannot show the way by scent tracks.

While some of the workers that first reach the food source maintain the blockade operation, another group does not join the war immedi-

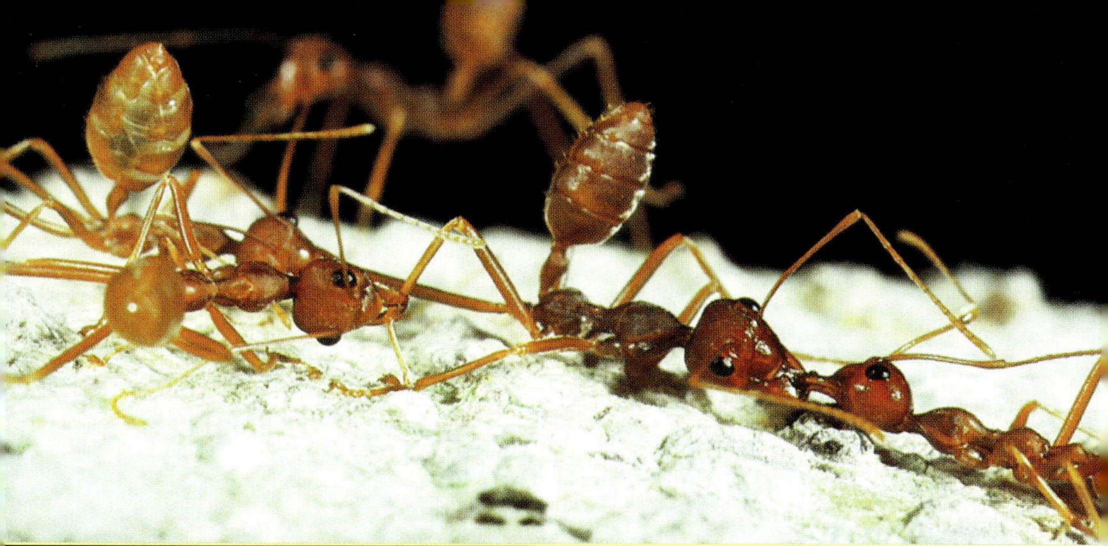
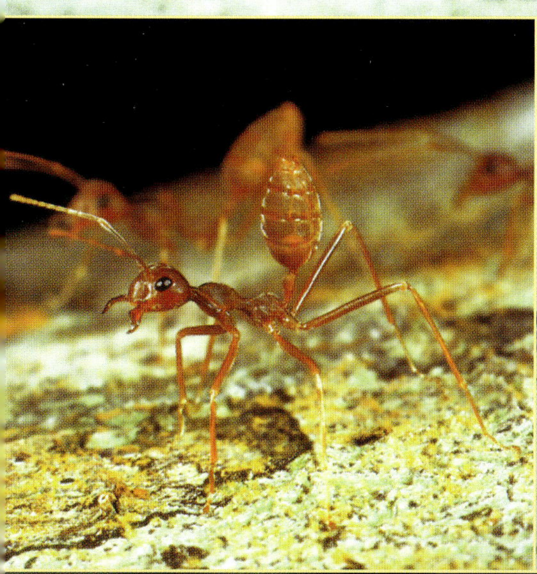
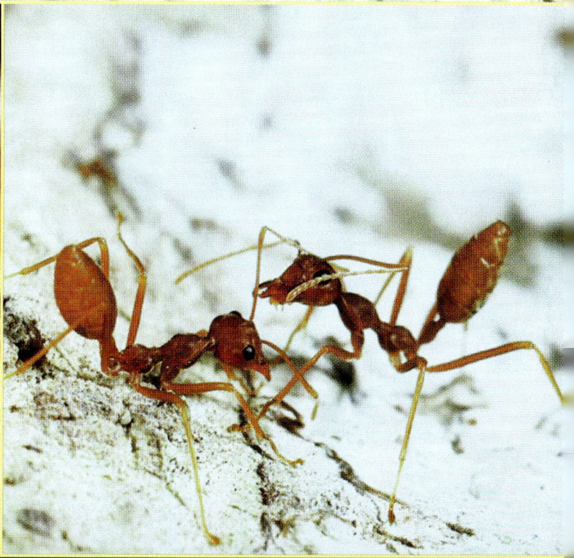
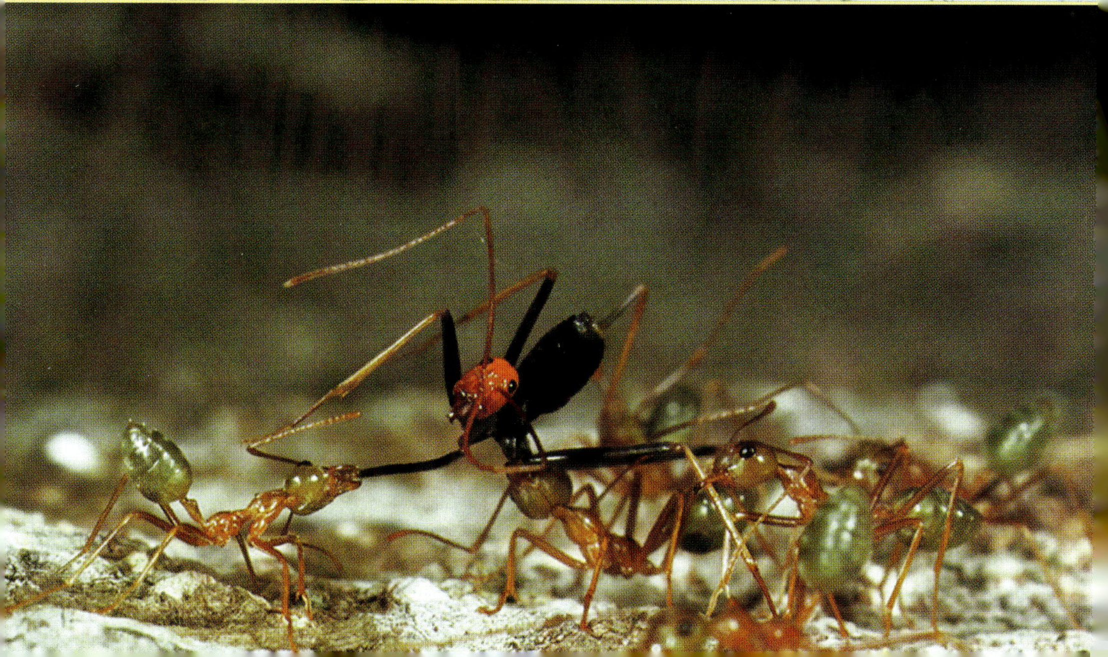

ately, preferring to return home, and leaving scent tracks. When they arrive home, they warn their nest mates by moving their bodies back and forth, and touching the antennae of the other ants with their own antennae. With this smart tactic, reinforcements are gathered for the fighting workers.

Apart from ordinary sieges during the day, the ants become so aggressive during a famine that they may destroy each other completely. One colony may destroy another completely within 10-14 days.

Another cause of war is one colony entering the territory of another. Ants mark their territories with a pheromone. When another colony comes to the area, it notices this pheromone and normally does not settle here. But if it does, this will be a cause of war.

In such situations, for instance, weaver ants run to the nearest leaf while leaving a secretion behind. When they find their nest mates, they tell them about the fight by their movements. Their mates start moving upon this invitation and travel towards the war zone following the workers. In half an hour, more than one hundred ants reach the arena.

In short, ant colonies lead a sophisticated existence with their natural boundaries, security and information systems against danger and armies that are strong enough to defend the whole colony. To found such a system and to have the colony members adopt the system, an intelligent and conscious will and education are needed. Yet, there is no apparent planner and no apparent education. The system has been designed by an invisible will and has been bestowed upon all ants when they first arrive on earth. In other words, Allah Who has created the ants has chosen a complex defence system for them and has inspired in the ants the program needed for performance of this system.

Now let us see the details of this system, which is an open system of creation.

Defence Tactics

In wars among different colonies, there are certain tactics resorted to by ants. They walk about with legs stretched out in a stiltlike posture while lifting their heads and abdomens and occasionally inflating their abdomens to a slight degree. The total effect is to make each ant appear larger than it really is.[72]

Above and below are seen ants that try to seem taller and bigger than they actually are.

Another defence tactic they use is "pacifying the enemy". An ant species (S. Invoila) gives out a venom during a fight by vibrating its belly and opening up its mandible slowly. Its enemies, who try to protect themselves from the venom open their jaws and drop some sugar water onto the open jaw of the venomous ant. The reason is that the venomous ant's aggression decreases when it has access to food. In short, the object is to draw the attention of the other side somewhere else and pacify it.

Tactics, of course, are not limited to these. The ants use many more sophisticated techniques in the war zones with the physical features they have and the intelligence that has been inspired in them.

Acid Producing Ants

Another very important defence technique of ants is their producing in the venom sacs in their bodies venom or formic acid as required. They use the venom they produce in a very successful way against their enemies. They can even have an effect on human beings with their venom. When they sting, they cause allergy shocks in certain people. Formic acid is, too, used effectively in chasing away the enemy.

If we accept evolution, we then have to admit that primitive ants did not start out with a poisoning system in their bodies, it having been formed somehow later on through the process of evolution. Yet this is a hypothesis against logic because, for the poisoning system to work, both the venom itself and the organ to keep it in have to be formed. It is necessary for this organ to have an insulated structure to prevent the dispersal of the venom to other parts of the body. Furthermore, an insulated pipe that extends from this organ to the mouth of the ant must exist. But this is not all. A muscle system or a mechanical arrangement has to exist which will allow this venom to be spurted on to the enemy (In fact, a separate gland is needed also to "lubricate" that area for the rotation of the abdominal section from which the venom is squirted).

These organs could not have developed gradually through the process of evolution because, if even one piece were lacking, this would render the system unworkable and cause the ant's death. Therefore there is just one explanation: The "chemical defence system" in question must have been in place from the moment the ants came into existence.

This in turn proves that a conscious design also exists and its other name is "Creation".

Another question to which evolutionists cannot find the answer is how – apart from their using this venom without any harm coming to themselves - they have learned to produce such a poison in their bodies (in venom sacks). In fact, the answer is very clear and obvious: Like all creatures in the universe, these ants with their perfect systems have been created all at the one time. The One Who has created the venom production centre in their bodies and Who has inspired them to use it in the most logical manner is Allah, the Creator of the worlds.

Ants Who Can Count

How is a simple insect able to assess the strength of the enemy? Interestingly enough, this is realized by the mathematical knowledge of the ant.

There are several ways the ant workers might indirectly assess the enemy strength. One of them is that they can "count heads" while shifting from one combatant to another. If their nestmates outnumber the enemy – say three to one – they will be subjectively aware of the imbalance in their favor and more inclined to press forward. If the reverse, they will retreat. A second method is to poll the enemy. If a high percentage of the alien workers encountered are majors, the other colony is probably large, because majors are produced in high numbers only when colonies approach maturity.[73]

Walking Bombs

The ultimate sacrifice in public service is to destroy enemies by committing suicide in defense of the colony. Many kinds of ants are prepared to assume this kamikaze role in one way or another, but none more dramatically than workers of a species of *Camponotus* of the saundersi group living in the rain forests of Malaysia.

Discovered in 1970 by two entomologists, these ants are anatomically and behaviorally programmed to be walking bombs. Two huge glands, filled with toxic secretions, run from the bases of the mandibles all the way to the posterior tip of the body. When the ants are pressed hard during combat, either by enemy ants or by an attacking predator, they contract their abdominal muscles violently, bursting open the body wall and spraying the secretions onto the foe.[74]

Such a serious sacrifice by the ants cannot, of course, be explained by either natural selection or by the "evolutionist socialization process". As emphasized many times before, the creature which carries out this very important sacrifice is not a man of a certain intelligence, education, sense and conscience, but an ant. Even if we think that ants may have gone through some physical change – there are ant fossils nevertheless that have remained unchanged for 80 million years – it is quite obvious that physical changes alone would not equip it with such features. No mutation experienced by a living being can cause its sudden transformation into a thinking, judging, feeling and sensing individual.

Even if we assumed that there had been an ant one day who decided to sacrifice itself to put up such a defence, it would of course be impossible for it to load this idea into its genes and transmit it to other ants.

Slave Trading Ants

The relationship between (*Formica Subintegra*), the parasitic ant and its slave (*Formica Subserica*) is interesting because it indicates the effect of chemical signals on the social lives of ants. "Slavery" is one of the intelligent war tactics of ants and maybe the most interesting one.[75]

Sometimes, if the soldiers of a colony realize that they can easily crush another colony, they may start hunting for slaves. They invade the nest of the other colony, kill the queen and take as loot the nectar-filled "honey pots" – those ants that fill their bodies with nectar. The most important point is their stealing the larvae of the queen. These larvae later on turn into young ants which will become "slave ants." They will look after the growing children of the colony queen and will search for and store food for the dominant colony.

When parasite ants attack another ant colony, the reason that the soldiers of the other colony cannot prevent the theft of their eggs and cocoons is a type of pheromone given out by the parasite ants. This pheromone is similar to a warning substance that exists in that colony and when it is secreted in large quantity by parasite ants, it results in the ants' running away instead of protecting their colonies.

As we know, there is a different pheromone secreted by each ant species. These pheromones are used for the designation of boundaries, the obtaining of information on the location and size of the enemy, as an attack command during war and as an alarm system.

Here there is a very interesting point. Parasite ants know the panic alarm of the enemy ant colony. They simulate this alarm and use it for a certain purpose. As a result, the enemy colony loses its present discipline because of the imitation pheromone secreted by the parasite ant, and runs away in panic without resorting to its defence system. That is, parasite ants cause the collapse of the enemy defence system by using very smart tactics. A masterfully prepared war strategy has come into operation. Furthermore, parasite ants have had all the chemical production and information infrastructure necessary for the implementation of this strategy since birth – since the time of their creation.

Some ant species lead their lives by having their slaves do everything for them. The red Amazon ant (*Polyergus*) is an example. All Amazon ants are soldiers. They have large sharp mandibles made for war. They can neither gather food nor look after babies. These ants attack the nests of certain small-sized black ant species and steal their cocoons and larvae. Ants emerging from cocoons are carried home to take on the jobs of the Amazon ants and stay with the Amazon colony, even if their own

The most important feature of slave trading ants is to steal the larvae of the colony they fight, and to make these larvae "slaves" for their own colonies. Above, an ant capturing the larva of the competitor colony is seen.

Slave trading ants do not steal only larvae from the competitor colony. Honey ants also steal the "honey pots" of the other colony and take them to their own nests.

nests are nearby. In fact, when Amazon ants have to migrate, they have these slaves do all the moving work, thus they are able to move very fast.[76]

Ants can defend themselves against even very large living beings due to their ability to leave traces. A good example of this is the ant's struggle with the dragon fly. Ants who spot the dragon fly gather together thanks to their tracing systems, then they attack and kill it. In another example, they are able by the same method to beat a caterpillar that attacks another member of the colony even if it is much larger in size than themselves.

It may seem normal for one living being to attack another or to fight with it for the purpose of defending its life, or for food. However, if a creature is acting together with others in its species while fighting the enemy, and if they communicate war tactics to each other, then we must inevitably focus on this subject.

To decide upon tactics, to fight accordingly with a certain order and discipline, and to use a communication system to protect such order and discipline, are all acts that need intelligence, planning and judgement. For instance, today's war strategies have been determined on the basis of the life-long experience of human beings. Army officers go through training in academies to learn such tactics. They also need specifically developed communication systems for the implementation of their strategies.

However, the soldiers that we talked about above, who determine the discipline and attack tactics with chemical communication systems, who attack the enemy together and who, if necessary, sacrifice themselves at times for other individuals of the army have not had any training and do not have any accumulation of information. These beings we are talking about are ants that are only a few milimetres long and do not have the ability to think.

MASTERS OF CAMOUFLAGE

The secret of the ant species *"Basiceros"* was not solved until recently. Researchers had come across these only once and had never found any ant similar to them again. Therefore, they were thought to be a very rare species.

However, a researcher solved the secret of these ants in 1985. He found out that they are not a species that is rarely found at all. The researcher, named La Selva, who solved this secret, described the *Basiceros* ants as master illusionists, because they were able to become "invisible" whenever they wanted.

What was it that made them invisible?

The *Basiceros* species, unlike other ant species, are covered with two layers of hair with splintered ends. When they walk on the ground, all kinds of dust, earth and bits of straws, etc., stick on these hairs. Another difference between these and other ants is that they do not clean the dirt off their bodies very often. Therefore, as shown in the pictures, they display total harmony with the environment they are in. When looked at from outside, it is almost impossible to locate them. They only become a little visible when they start walking. Yet, even in this case, they take precautions to protect themselves from birds, lizards and even the human eye. They are the sluggish ants in the world and may be observed to stand perfectly still for minutes at a time when they are disturbed.[77]

The camouflage technique applied by this ant species is very striking, because it is impossible for an ant to have developed a defence system by determining all its physiological characteristics by itself. All these features (body covered with hair, not cleaning often unlike other ants and moving very slowly) must have been defined beforehand so that the ant came into this world already equipped with the characteristics discussed.

As a result, again, we are facing a great truth. This ant species has also been created by Allah with all its features designated beforehand, thus showing us His attribute of Creator.

In the pictures on the left and above we see the master of camouflage of the ant world. The bodies of these ants of the *Basiceros* species are covered with two layers of hair with splintered ends. Thus, it is impossible to locate them.

RESERVING THE RACE

A large portion of an ant colony is made up of female ants. Male ants have a rather shorter life span. Their only task is to mate when they mature with a young queen. Male ants die a short while after they mate. All worker ants are female. In short, all ant communities are, in fact, a world of mothers and daughters.

Ants are a harmonious society regardless of their number. In ant colonies, it is possible to see every stage in the life of a society. The purpose in life for ants, who are bound to their colonies with great sacrifice is not individual. They are, all together, like a single body and their purpose is to keep that body alive. They do not think twice before electing death, if it is for the survival of the colony. The best example of this is what happens to the male ants after the nuptial flight.

Dying for Survival of the Race

The mating of ants looks almost like a ceremony. Most ants mate in the air. The males come earlier and wait for the young queen. When a female lands on the ground (the female also has wings before mating), 5-6 male ants start racing around the queen. When the female has obtained enough sperms, it sends out a certain vibration. The male understands this signal as meaning that the female is ready to detach. A short while after mating, the male ant dies.[78]

This type of sacrifice is in fact very hard to explain. The male ant taking the nuptial flight which will end in its death for the survival of its race is a type of behaviour that cannot be explained by the theory of evolution because, according to the fundamental logic of evolution, each living being only worries about the continuation of its own life. Yet, male ants have been fertilizing female ants for millions of years, knowing that at the end, death is inevitable.

The only truth that can explain this sacrifice is that the male ant acts under the inspiration of its Creator. Otherwise, it is impossible that a creature, which is alleged to go through the natural selection process, should preserve such sacrificial behaviour for millions of years. Judging by the basic principles of the theory of evolution, male ants would have to escape from this "death flight" one way or another, and this would mean the end of the ant species. Yet, currently, thousands of ant species still keep on living on earth with their colonies numbering hundreds of thousands. Not a single male ant has ever run away from this flight which means "the end" for it.

After the Nuptial Flight

After mating, the female ant looks for a suitable nest, and when she finds one, she enters it and promptly tears off her wings. Later on, she bars the entrance and stays without food and alone for several weeks. Then she lays her eggs. (During this time, she feeds on her wings). She feeds the larvae coming out first with her own saliva. This long-lasting and tough effort is another example of sacrifice, but in the remaining portion of her life, the queen will be fed by her colony.

Due to limited food, the first herd is small. These are the first workers of the colony and take care of the following herds continuing to make sacrifices in the same way. The new generation of ants that grows up under their exceptional care become larger, because they have better nutrition.

First Founders of Sperm Bank

As we mentioned before, the lives of male ants are not very long. They die anything from a few hours to a couple of days after the nuptial flight. Yet, it is very interesting that each male who has taken the nuptial flight, risking death, has left sperms for its offspring to be born years after it dies. Well, how are these sperms preserved alive and how are they able to produce new ants by fertilizing the eggs? Can the ants have developed a superior technology and formed a sperm bank?

Above are ants during nuptial flight. On the left are seen female ants before the nuptial flight.

Yes, each queen ant has a sperm bank in her body. After receiving the ejaculate from the male, the queen stores it in an oval bag located near the tip of her abdomen. In this organ, called the spermatheca, the individual sperm are physiologically inactivated, and they can remain in suspended animation for years. When at last the queen lets them back out into her reproductive tract, either one at a time or in small groups, they become agile again and ready to fertilize the egg passing down the tract from the ovaries.[79] This means that the sperm bank which has come into use over the last 25 years through high technology, has been used by the ants since time immemorial.

This mechanism of which, until 50 years ago, human beings had not the slightest inkling, has been used by ants for millions of years. Since the ants cannot go through stages man has gone through by setting up laboratories and having this mechanism placed in their bodies, they must have had this mechanism since the very beginning. If allegations are made to the contrary, many questions similar to the ones below shall have to be answered.

1. When the ants came into existence for the first time, did not the males die after the nuptial flight? If they did not, then why are they dying now? Did they think that it was more appropriate to be destroyed after the death flight as part of the survival of the fittest process?

2. Since male ants die right after the nuptial flight, would not the ant species have been extinct long time ago had it not been for the formation of the sperm storage required for the survival of their species?

3. If the sperm bank has existed since they first came into existence, then who has equipped their bodies with this mechanism?

After the nuptial flight, the queen looks for a suitable place to found her colony. When she finds a place like she wants, she first tears off her wings and starts forming her own colony by reproducing.

These are just a few of the questions that must be answered by those who do not accept the supreme creation by the Creator. Thousands more questions may be formulated just on the subject of the survival of the ant species and each one of these questions points to creation by design and renders evolutionist claims impossible.

Sacrifice of Workers

The eggs that the queen ant lays and immature young ants both live in the child care chambers of the nest. If the temperature and humidity become such that they may harm the young, then worker ants carry the eggs and the young ants to a more suitable environment. They keep the eggs close to the surface in the daytime to benefit from the heat and take them to deeper chambers at night or on rainy days.

This means that the workers try to protect the eggs and young ants with great care and try to keep them comfortable. Some of them take the larvae around the nest on a hot day to cool them down and some of them cover the walls of the nest with discarded cocoons to prevent humidity and some of them seek food. Every single one of these actions shows that ants act out of very kind consideration. One ant will take the larvae around the nest to cool them, while another ant will insulate the wall of the nest by cocoons to adjust the temperature – a very modern insulation technique. Yet, it must not be forgotten that this being which we regard as having made a kind gesture, does not have any thinking capacity. Regardless of how advanced its technology may become, science will never be able to find the cause of this sacrifice displayed by a tiny bug. Furthermore, this sacrifice is in total contradiction of the most fundamental principles of the theory of evolution.

All these examples show that these living beings also act under Allah's inspiration and that they obey Him. This secret is explained in the Qur'an as follows:

> **Everything in the heavens and every creature on the earth prostrates to Allah, as do the angels. They are not puffed up with pride. They fear their Lord above them and do everything they are ordered to do. (Surat an-Nahl: 49-50)**

The sole task of one group of worker ants in ant colonies is to look after the eggs and larvae. These workers are generous with their time. They spend every moment of their lives guaranteeing the survival of their species.

For worker ants, the maintenance of the eggs are very important. Above, worker ants that look after the queen's eggs are seen.

Treasure of Ants

All the activities of ant colonies centre on the queen and her eggs. The ants hold their queens, who ensure the reproduction of their colonies, in high regard. All their needs are met by worker ants. The most important thing a worker ant does is to serve the queen and ensure her survival and her babies.

Ant eggs are the most valuable treasure of the colony. The first thing the ants do when they sense any danger to their larvae is to take the babies to a secure place. Yet, since baby ants die within a couple of hours of coming into contact with the dry air outside, worker ants try to keep the air humid in the sections where the larvae are. There are various techniques they have developed for this. First of all, they build their nests in such a way as to keep the humidity of the air and of the soil at appropriate levels. In addition, ants who assume the task of being caretakers of the babies, move the immature ants up and down in the structure. They try to find the most suitable environment for them. Furthermore, the needs of baby ants vary according to age. For instance, while eggs and larvae need a humid environment, the ants in the pupa phase have to be in a strictly dry medium. Workers keep on working for 24 hours without rest to complete these tasks.[80]

The worker ants in the colony have dedicated themselves to raising the eggs of their constantly laying queen instead of laying eggs themselves. They take many risks on this score, because the humid medium required for eggs and larvae is ideal for the growth of bacteria and fungi that are potential health hazards for the ants.

Then, how are the workers protected in such an unhealthy environment? Allah, Who has created ants with their magnificent systems, has given them another defence technique. The metapleural glands in the thorax of adult ants continuously secrete substances that kill bacteria and fungi. Therefore, ant colonies are rarely struck by bacterial or fungal infections.[81]

Can Darwinism Explain Sacrifice?

Charles Darwin, who is the originator of the theory of evolution, has suggested that the basic motivation of the process of evolution was that of staying alive. In Darwin's view, when individuals of a species acquire traits that increase their chances for survival, those individuals have an advantage; due to this advantage, they survive and produce relatively more living offspring, thus eventually spreading the trait throughout their species. Evolution, therefore, would be expected to favor self-preservation, not self-sacrifice.[82]

Yet, Darwin's theory of natural selection was given a shattering blow by the discovery of so many incredible examples of self-sacrifice shown by ants. It was very difficult for proponents of the theory of evolution to produce an explanation of such characteristics, some of which were found while Darwin was still alive. In fact, Darwin himself stated in his book, called The Origin of Species:

> Many instincts are so wonderful that their development will probably appear to the reader a difficulty sufficient to overthrow my whole theory. I may here premise that I have nothing to do with the origin of the mental powers, any more than I have with that of life itself. [83]

After such an open confession, the hypothesis he set forth in order to save his theory is beset by even greater complications. According to the explanation Darwin brought to this conflicting situation, natural selection was realized not at the level of individual, but at the group level within certain groups.

However, this could not go any further than a claim impossible to prove, because it was just an estimate which was set forth for the sake of saving the theory, which did not depend on any solid findings or observations. Evolutionists who came after Darwin could never explain the examples of sacrifice in animals.

It is impossible to explain the examples of sacrifice and generosity experienced among ants, termites, bees and other social insects by any technique offered by the theory of evolution. There is only a single explanation for a living being to put its own security and comfort at risk in order to work on providing security and comfort for members of the group it lives in: the social order of the group has been determined by a conscious designer and this designer has assigned different tasks for each member of the group. The members of the group abide by this task distribution and if necessary, sacrifice themselves. What is important is the survival of the order of the group, and the sacrifice needed for it may be achieved, not by the will of insects lacking any consciousness and judgement, but by the will that directs them.

FEEDING AND HUNTING

Each living being uses different methods to satisfy its needs for food. In this chapter, you are going to read about the tactics used by ants when looking for food, about their communications and the competition among them to get to the food. All the tactics tried by such a small creature to obtain its food shows, as in previous chapters, the greatness, magnificence and power of Allah, the "Supreme Possessor of Intelligence" Who has created them.

How is a "family" with a population in hundreds of thousands fed? One of the most important things needed for survival of the colony is resolving of the food problem, and each ant in the colony has its share of this responsibility.

As they do in other aspects of their lives, the ants carry out systematic work in solving the nutrition problem. Old worker ants are sent out as explorers to survey the land around the nest to find food resources for the colony which has a population of hundreds of thousands (sometimes millions). When explorer ants find a food source, they gather their nest mates around the food in numbers which depend on the size and richness of the source. Ants solve the food problem by a very strong communication network and their generosity, which never says "Only me".

Ants That Feed Each Other

Ants of different species try not to get in each other's way while looking for food. Each one determines a path for itself to get to the food source. If ants go into another colony's territory by mistake, this becomes a declaration of war. In such a situation, explorer ants come back to the nest right away and close the nest entrance and all colony members come together to defend their colonies against danger.

Then, how do the ants feed during this fight, when they have no opportunity to bring in food?

At this point, a feature of the ants that distinguishes them from other living beings emerges. During this period when they cannot search for food, all colony members feed on the food stored in the crops of young workers.

In fact, this sharing technique is one they use all their lives, and not only at special times. Ants not only carry the food globules stored in their bodies, but they feed each other mouth to mouth. Once a hunter returns home loaded with liquid food, it shakes its head to the right and left to attract the attention of its mates standing still or goes directly to its mates and presents the food globule in its fully opened jaw to them.[84] This liquid food exchange, done by a reflux from the crop which provides quick distribution of the food to the colony is, in fact, quite an impressive example of sharing. Also husks and seeds brought to the nest are consumed as well by all of the ants together. Thus, the food requirement of the whole colony is satisfied without any problems.

This system is one that makes it necessary to admit of the existence of a supreme designer. It is a reality that a chain of random events cannot form such a storage system so complex and requiring great sacrifice. What is more, each ant comes to this world knowing this system. That is, the necessity to share its food has been ingrained in it before its birth and not after. Not only has this sense of sacrifice been inspired in it, but because a special mechanism is needed to present the food it has saved in its crop, its body structure has been designed to make this sharing possible. This sharing event realized among ant colonies once again renders the word "chance" insufficient or even meaningless, due to the sense of self-sacrifice being much in evidence. As we have emphasized many times before, the theory of evolution assumes the existence of a full-fledged competition and life struggle among all living things. Therefore, examples of self-sacrifice among ant species are acts most difficult to explain. Ants living under a feeding system based on sharing are proof that they do not act in the way suggested by the theory of evolution. They are not engaging in a random "fight for survival" but are rather performing the duties given to them (according to the Qur'an "revealed to them") and thus they are able to transform their colonies with hundreds of thousands or even millions of members into a true civilization.

In the Qur'an, in surat an-Nahl, Allah describes the "revelation" that makes it obligatory for the animals to perform certain tasks given to them by Him:

> **And your Lord revealed to the bee: "Build dwellings in the mountains and the trees and also in the structures which men erect. Then eat from every kind of fruit and travel the paths of your Lord, which have been made easy for you to follow." From inside them comes a drink of varying colours, containing healing for mankind. There is certainly a sign in that for people who reflect. (Surat an-Nahl: 68-69)**

The Qur'an, of course, does not list the animals' special duties through Allah's inspiration one by one. The honey bee is just one example. Yet, when we look at the ant, we can see that this small being, which performs as perfect tasks as the honey bee, and which is at least as generous, social and loyal, acts under a similar revelation.

Rational Techniques in Carrying Food

The discovery by approximately 8800 known ant species of the food sources they need, and their carrying them to their homes are done by different methods. In certain species, ants hunt on their own and carry the food individually. Yet in others, hunting is done as a group and they carry and defend their food together.

If the food they find is in suitable dimensions for them, ants usually carry it alone. If the food is too large for a single ant to carry or if it is in small piles, all within a particular area, they give out a poisonous hormone to prevent others from coming into the territory. Then they go to call other workers, large and small, to carry the food.

The perfect division of labour governing the lives of ants is observed here also. Large ants tear up the food and defend it against strangers, while smaller ones take care of carrying the pieces home. A worker lifts the food with its jaw and keeps it in front of it while returning home. When there is a group, the substance they can carry becomes even larger. They lift the food by using one or two legs. At the same time, they bite the food, opening their jaws. Workers apply different techniques, depending on their positions and their directions. Those in front walk backwards, pulling the food. Those at the back walk forward, pushing it, and those at the sides give support. By this technique, it is possible to carry weights many times greater than what a single ant can carry. In fact, it has been observed that ants acting in unison can carry a weight 5,000 times as heavy as that carried by a single worker. 100 ants can carry a large worm at ground level, moving it 0.4 cm per second.

Ants and Scent Tracks

Communication by tracks (following of scent tracks) is a technique that is commonly used by ants. There are many interesting examples on the subject:

An ant species living in American deserts secretes a special scent produced in its venom sac if it realizes that the dead bug it has found is too wide or heavy to carry or drag. Its nest mates far away detect the scent and start moving towards its source. When ants have gathered around the victim in sufficient numbers to carry it, they start carrying it towards the nest.

When the fire ants separate from home in search of food, they follow the scent track for a short while and then they leave each other and search on their own. Their having found the food source becomes apparent from the way they behave. When the fire ant discovers food, it returns to its nest at a slower speed with its body quite close to the ground. It sticks out its needle at certain intervals and the end of the nee-

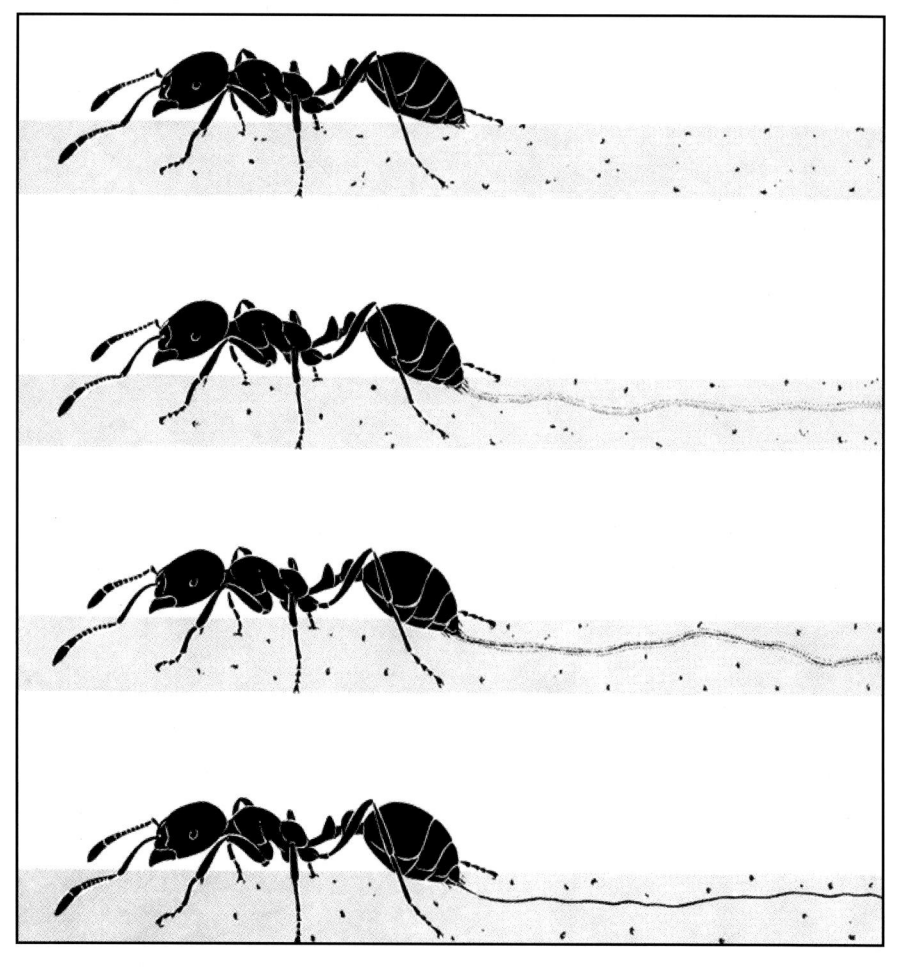

An ant finding a food source leaves a chemical trace on the ground with the needle at its rear. This trace helps its nest mates reach the food source.

dle touches the ground like a pencil drawing a thin line. Thus, it leaves a trace behind it that leads to the food.[85]

Ants Who Serve As Compasses

Food-seeking ants carry out a task in a manner which is very hard to explain. They go to the food source following a wiggly path, but when they return home, it is via a short and straight line. Then, how is it that ants that can see only a few centimetres ahead of themselves, march in such a straight line?

To find an answer to this question, a researcher called Richard Feynman placed a clump of sugar at one end of the bathtub, then waited for an ant to come and find it. As this pioneer ant returned home with news of the feast, Feynman followed the wiggly path it followed. He then traced the path of each successive ant to follow the trail. The successive ants, he found, did not stick exactly to the trail; they did better, cutting corners until the trail became a straight line.

Later on, inspired by Feynman, a computer scientist, Alfred Bruckstein, proved mathematically that successive followers really do make a wiggly line straight. The conclusion he arrived at was the same: after a certain number of ants, the path length shrinks to some minimum value: to the shortest possible distance between two points - namely, a straight line.[86]

What we talked about above is of course, something which would require great skill on the part of a human being because he would certainly need to use a compass, a watch and at times much more complex instruments for any distance relative to his own dimensions and would have to have a perfect knowledge of mathematics. In contrast to this, the guide an ant has in exploring on its own is the sun, while its compass is the position of branches and other natural landmarks. Later on, ants remember their shapes and can thus find the shortest route to their nests although they have never had any prior knowledge of it.

This is very easy to say but very hard to explain! How can these tiny living beings do such calculations when they have neither a brain nor the capacity to think and judge?

Imagine that you leave a man in an unfamiliar forest. Even if he knows the direction to go, he will have a hard time finding his way and will probably get lost. In the meantime, it will be necessary for him to look around carefully and think about which would be the best way to go. Yet, ants act as if they are encoded on the matter of path finding. In the evening, they can easily find and follow the road they took to find the food in the morning, even if all the conditions have changed.

The Perfect Hunting Technique

Certain ant species use their teeth to eat spider eggs, caterpillars, insects and termites. Many ants (for example *Dacetine*) specialize in non-winged insects. These insects live in groups in the ground and in decayed leaves. The bugs have extensions under their bodies in the form of folded forks. When they rock and get up, this organ throws them into the air and forward like a miniature kangaroo. Dacetine ants use their jaws like an animal-catching trap against this very effective manoeuvre. When the food-seeking ant receives the scent of an insect with its antennae, it lies in wait, opening its jaws 180 degrees. It locks the small teeth in its jaw by pressing onto its upper palate. It inspects its surroundings by moving its antennae forward. Then the ant approaches the insect slowly. When its antennae touch it, the little insect is at a distance where its lower jaw teeth can reach it. When the ant lowers its palate, the jaw suddenly shuts down and the insect is squeezed between the teeth as if impaled.[87]

The above-mentioned ants never miss their prey, because they have jaws with the fastest reflex in the world.

Our speed of blinking the eye is very slow compared to the biting speed of the trapper ant. While the opening and closing of the eyelid takes about one third of a second, the jaws of these ants (Odontomachus bawi) work almost 100 times faster. The fastest hit observed took in 0.33 milliseconds.[88]

The jaw structures of trapper ants are approximately 1.8 milimetre long. In the interior sections, there is a sac full of air attached to the trachea. This system ensures exceptionally fast movement of the teeth. The jaws act as a miniature mouse trap. When hunting, the jaw is fully opened and ready to close any time. The biting speed slows down near the end of the biting process. To prevent the teeth hitting each other very hard, the jaw movement is slowed down by the special muscle system.[89]

It is impossible for such a hunting mechanism to have developed through evolution. That is, without conscious design and at random.

The only acceptable truth is that the power who has created the ants with all their miraculous characteristics and perfect life styles is Allah, Who is sovereign over all of nature and the universe.

Harun Yahya

CONCLUSION

We have given you some examples of the effects of Allah's art of creation on a living species only a few centimetres long. It is correct to say "some examples" because there are hundreds more, relating to ants, which can be listed. However, each one of the listed examples is in itself a matter for profound reflection.

It must not be forgotten that life forms exist all over the earth. The life bestowed by Allah on small ants, which have a complicated system and an extensive range of activities, has also been created for living beings in each square milimetre. Single-celled organisms, insects, wild animals and plants are all created with perfect programming, like the ants.

All these miracles of creation are things which human beings do not even think about during their daily lives, or they just look at them without comprehending them.

With this book, we have tried to dispel the deep mist with which modern society covers the people's eyes. Our goal is to present anew the proof of Allah's eternal existence to those who have forgotten Him because they have been too preoccupied all their lives with worldly matters, such as jobs, houses, and financial concerns. It is also our goal to give to those who do think of Him, new material to reflect upon. Both these tasks are very important. And as a major step towards their fulfilment, we have analyzed in this text the miracles of creation, so that the One Who is the mastermind behind them may come to be known and appreciated. Allah explains the significance of this as follows in our only indicator of the true path, the Qur'an:

And the earth- We have spread it out, and set thereon mountains standing firm, and produced therefrom every kind of beautiful

growth (in pairs) - to be observed and commemorated by every devotee turning (to God). (Surah Qaf: 7-8)

Our goal is to have the readers think of the message of this book as a message "to be observed and commemorated". Therefore, rather than becoming submerged in the troubles of a society which has turned its back on Allah and forgotten Him, the reader should ponder deeply upon the existence and power of Allah and should rearrange his life in accordance with this truth.

Allah has created all the things He created to become acquainted with Him. Those who turn away from Him, despite this, deserve a great punishment.

THE EVOLUTION DECEIT

The theory of evolution is a philosophy and a conception of the world that produces false hypotheses, assumptions and imaginary scenarios in order to explain the existence and origin of life in terms of mere coincidences. The roots of this philosophy go back as far as antiquity and ancient Greece.

All atheist philosophies that deny creation, directly or indirectly embrace and defend the idea of evolution. The same condition today applies to all the ideologies and systems that are antagonistic to religion.

The evolutionary notion has been cloaked in a scientific disguise for the last century and a half in order to justify itself. Though put forward as a supposedly scientific theory during the mid-19th century, the theory, despite all the best efforts of its advocates, has not so far been verified by any scientific finding or experiment. Indeed, the "very science" on which the theory depends so greatly has demonstrated and continues to demonstrate repeatedly that the theory has no merit in reality.

Laboratory experiments and probabilistic calculations have definitely made it clear that the amino acids from which life arises cannot have been formed by chance. The cell, which supposedly emerged by chance under primitive and uncontrolled terrestrial conditions according to evolutionists, still cannot be synthesised even in the most sophisticated, high-tech laboratories of the 20th century. Not a single "transitional form", creatures which are supposed to show the gradual evolution of advanced organisms from more primitive ones as neo-Darwinist theory claims, has ever been found anywhere in the world despite the most diligent and prolonged search in the fossil record.

Striving to gather evidence for evolution, evolutionists have unwittingly proven by their own hands that evolution cannot have happened at all!

The person who originally put forward the theory of evolution, essentially in the form that it is defended today, was an amateur English biologist by the name of Charles Robert Darwin. Darwin first published his ideas in a book entitled *The Origin of Species by Means of Natural Selection* in 1859. Darwin claimed in his book that all living beings had a common ancestor and that they evolved from one another by means of natural selection. Those that best adapted to the habitat transferred their traits to subsequent generations, and by accumulating over great epochs, these advantageous qualities transformed individuals into totally different species from their ancestors. The human being was thus the most developed product of the mechanism of natural selection. In short, the origin of one species was another species.

Darwin's fanciful ideas were seized upon and promoted by certain ideological and political circles and the theory became very popular. The main reason was that the level of knowledge of those days was not yet sufficient to reveal that Darwin's imaginary scenarios were false. When Darwin put forward his assumptions, the disciplines of genetics, microbiology, and biochemistry did not yet exist. If they had, Darwin might easily have recognised that his theory was totally unscientific and thus would not have attempted to advance such meaningless claims: the information determining species already exists in the genes and it is impossible for natural selection to produce new species by altering genes.

While the echoes of Darwin's book reverberated, an Austrian botanist by the name of Gregor Mendel discovered the laws of inheritance in 1865. Although little known before the end of the century, Mendel's discovery gained great importance in the early 1900s with the birth of the science of genetics. Some time later, the structures of genes and chromosomes were discovered. The discovery, in the 1950s, of the DNA molecule, which incorporates genetic information, threw the theory of evolution into a great crisis, because the origin of the immense amount of information in DNA could not possibly be explained by coincidental happenings.

Besides all these scientific developments, no transitional forms, which were supposed to show the gradual evolution of living organisms from primitive to advanced species, have ever been found despite years of search.

These developments ought to have resulted in Darwin's theory being banished to the dustbin of history. However, it was not, because certain circles insisted on revising, renewing, and elevating the theory to a scientific platform. These efforts gain meaning only if we realise that behind the theory lie ideological intentions rather than scientific concerns.

Nevertheless, some circles that believed in the necessity of upholding a theory that had reached an impasse soon set up a new model. The name of this new model was neo-Darwinism. According to this theory, species evolved as a result of mutations, minor changes in their genes, and the fittest ones survived through the mechanism of natural selection. When, however, it was proved that the mechanisms proposed by neo-Darwinism were invalid and minor changes were not sufficient for the formation of living beings, evolutionists went on to look for new models. They came up with a new claim called "punctuated equilibrium" that rests on no rational or scientific grounds. This model held that living beings suddenly evolved into another species without any transitional forms. In other words, species with no evolutionary "ancestors" suddenly appeared. This was a way of describing creation, though evolutionists would be loath to admit this. They tried to cover it up with incomprehensible scenarios. For instance, they said that the first bird in history could all of a sudden inexplicably have popped out of a reptile egg. The same theory also held that carnivorous land-dwelling animals could have turned into giant whales, having undergone a sudden and comprehensive transformation.

Charles Darwin

These claims, totally contradicting all the rules of genetics, biophysics, and biochemistry are as scientific as fairy-tales of frogs turning into princes! Nevertheless, being distressed by the crisis that the neo-Darwinist assertion was in, some evolutionist paleontologists embraced this theory, which has the distinction of being even more bizarre than neo-Darwinism itself.

The only purpose of this model was to provide an explanation for the gaps in the fossil record that the neo-Darwinist model could not explain. However, it is hardly rational to attempt to explain the gap in the fossil record of the evolution of birds with a claim that "a bird popped all of a sudden out of a reptile egg", because, by the evolutionists' own admission, the evolution of a species to another species requires a great and advantageous change in genetic information. However, no mutation whatsoever improves the genetic information or adds new information to it. Mutations only derange genetic information. Thus, the "gross mutations" imagined by the punctuated equilibrium model, would only cause "gross", that is "great", reductions and impairments in the genetic information.

The theory of punctuated equilibrium was obviously merely a product of the imagination. Despite this evident truth, the advocates of evolution did not hesitate to honour this theory. The fact that the model of evolution proposed by Darwin could not be proved by the fossil record forced them to do so. Darwin claimed that species underwent a gradual change, which necessitated the existence of half-bird/half-reptile or half-fish/half-reptile freaks. However, not even one of these "transitional forms" was found despite the extensive studies of evolutionists and the hundreds of thousands of fossils that were unearthed.

Evolutionists seized upon the model of punctuated equilibrium with the hope of concealing this great fossil fiasco. As we have stated before, it was very evident that this theory is a fantasy, so it very soon consumed itself. The model of punctuated equilibrium was never put forward as a consistent model, but rather used as an escape in cases that plainly did not fit the model of gradual evolution. Since evolutionists today realise that complex organs such as eyes, wings, lungs, brain and others explicitly refute the model of gradual evolution, in these particular points they are compelled to take shelter in the fantastic interpretations of the model of punctuated equilibrium.

Is there any Fossil Record to Verify the Theory of Evolution?

The theory of evolution argues that the evolution of a species into another species takes place gradually, step-by-step over millions of years. The logical inference drawn from such a claim is that monstrous living organisms called "transitional forms" should have lived during these periods of transformation. Since evolutionists allege that all living things evolved from each other step-by-step, the number and variety of these transitional forms should have been in the millions.

If such creatures had really lived, then we should see their remains everywhere. In fact, if this thesis is correct, the number of intermediate transitional forms should be even greater than the number of animal species alive today and their fossilised remains should be abundant all over the world.

Since Darwin, evolutionists have been searching for fossils and the result has been for them a crushing disappointment. Nowhere in the world – neither on land nor in the depths of the sea – has any intermediate transitional form between any two species ever been uncovered.

Darwin himself was quite aware of the absence of such transitional forms. It was his greatest hope that they would be found in the future. Despite his hopefulness, he saw that the biggest stumbling block to his theory was the missing transitional forms. This is why, in his book *The Origin of Species*, he wrote:

> Why, if species have descended from other species by fine gradations, do we not everywhere see innumerable transitional forms? Why is not all nature in confusion, instead of the species being, as we see them, well defined?... But, as by this theory innumerable transitional forms must have existed, why do we not find them embedded in countless numbers in the crust of the earth?... But in the intermediate region, having intermediate conditions of life, why do we not now find closely-linking intermediate varieties? This difficulty for a long time quite confounded me.[90]

Darwin was right to be worried. The problem bothered other evolutionists as well. A famous British paleontologist, Derek V. Ager, admits this embarrassing fact:

> The point emerges that if we examine the fossil record in detail, whether

at the level of orders or of species, we find – over and over again – not gradual evolution, but the sudden explosion of one group at the expense of another.[91]

The gaps in the fossil record cannot be explained away by the wishful thinking that not enough fossils have yet been unearthed and that these missing fossils will one day be found. Another evolutionist paleontologist, T. Neville George, explains the reason:

> There is no need to apologise any longer for the poverty of the fossil record. In some ways, it has become almost unmanageably rich and discovery is outpacing integration... The fossil record nevertheless continues to be composed mainly of gaps.[92]

Life Emerged on Earth Suddenly and in Complex Forms

When terrestrial strata and the fossil record are examined, it is seen that living organisms appeared simultaneously. The oldest stratum of the earth in which fossils of living creatures have been found is that of the "Cambrian", which has an estimated age of 530-520 million years.

Living creatures that are found in the strata belonging to the Cambrian period emerged in the fossil record all of a sudden without any pre-existing ancestors. The vast mosaic of living organisms, made up of such great numbers of complex creatures, emerged so suddenly that this miraculous event is referred to as the "Cambrian Explosion" in scientific literature.

Most of the organisms found in this stratum have highly advanced organs like eyes, or systems seen in organisms with a highly advanced organisation such as gills, circulatory systems, and so on. There is no sign in the fossil record to indicate that these organisms had any ancestors. Richard Monestarsky, the editor of *Earth Sciences* magazine, states about the sudden emergence of living species:

> A half-billion years ago the remarkably complex forms of animals that we see today suddenly appeared. This moment, right at the start of Earth's Cambrian Period, some 550 million years ago, marks the evolutionary explosion that filled the seas with the world's first complex creatures. The large animal phyla of today were present already in the early Cambrian and they were as distinct from each other then as they are today.[93]

**The Most Cherished Pieces of Evidence
of Evolution are Proven to be Invalid**
A four hundred and ten million-year-old Coelacanth fish fossil (right). Evolutionists claimed that it was the transitional form proving the transition of this fish from water to land. The fact that more than forty living examples of this fish have been caught in the last fifty years reveals that this is still a perfectly ordinary fish and that it is still living. A one hundred and thirty-five million-year-old Archaeopteryx fossil, the alleged ancestor of birds, which is said to have evolved from dinosaurs (above). Research on the fossil showed it, on the contrary, to be an extinct bird that had once flown but later lost that ability.

Not being able to find answers to the question of how earth came to overflow with thousands of different animal species, evolutionists posit an imaginary period of 20 million years before the Cambrian Period to explain how life originated and "the unknown happened". This period is called the "evolutionary gap". No evidence for it has ever been found and the concept is still conveniently nebulous and undefined even today.

In 1984, numerous complex invertebrates were unearthed in Chengjiang, set in the central Yunnan plateau in the high country of southwest China. Among them were trilobites, now extinct, but no less complex in structure than any modern invertebrate.

The Swedish evolutionist paleontologist, Stefan Bengston, explains the situation as follows:

> If any event in life's history resembles man's creation myths, it is this sudden diversification of marine life when multicellular organisms took over as the dominant actors in ecology and evolution. Baffling (and embarrassing) to Darwin, this event still dazzles us.[94]

The sudden appearance of these complex living beings with no predecessors is no less baffling (and embarrassing) for evolutionists today than it was for Darwin 135 years ago. In nearly a century and a half, they have advanced not one step beyond the point that stymied Darwin.

As may be seen, the fossil record indicates that living things did not evolve from primitive to advanced forms, but instead emerged all of a sudden and in a perfect state. The absence of the transitional forms is not peculiar to the Cambrian period. Not a single transitional form verifying the alleged evolutionary "progression" of vertebrates – from fish to amphibians, reptiles, birds, and mammals – has ever been found. Every living species appears instantaneously and in its current form, perfect and complete, in the fossil record.

In other words, living beings did not come into existence through evolution. They were created.

EVOLUTION FORGERIES
Deceptions in Drawings

The fossil record is the principal source for those who seek evidence for the theory of evolution. When inspected carefully and without prejudice, the fossil record refutes the theory of evolution rather than supporting it. Nevertheless, misleading interpretations of fossils by evolutionists and their prejudiced representation to the public have given many people the impression that the fossil record indeed supports the theory of evolution.

The susceptibility of some findings in the fossil record to all kinds of interpretations is what best serves the evolutionists' purposes. The fossils unearthed are most of the time unsatisfactory for reliable identification. They usually consist of scattered, incomplete bone fragments. For this reason, it is very easy to distort the available data and to use it as desired. Not surprisingly, the reconstructions (drawings and models) made by evolutionists based on such fossil remains are prepared entirely speculatively in order to confirm evolutionary theses. Since people are readily affected by visual information, these imaginary reconstructed models are employed to convince them that the reconstructed creatures really existed in the past.

Evolutionist researchers draw human-like imaginary creatures, usually setting out from a single tooth, or a mandible fragment or a humerus, and present them to the public in a sensational manner as if they were links in human evolution. These drawings have played a great role in the establishment of the image of "primitive men" in the minds of many people.

These studies based on bone remains can only reveal very general characteristics of the creature concerned. The distinctive details are present in the soft tissues that quickly vanish with time. With the soft tissues speculatively interpreted, everything becomes possible within the boundaries of the imagination of the reconstruction's producer. Earnst A. Hooten from Harvard University explains the situation like this:

False fossil: Piltdown Man

> To attempt to restore the soft parts is an even more hazardous undertaking. The lips, the eyes, the ears, and the nasal tip leave no clues on the underlying bony parts. You can with equal facility model on a Neanderthaloid skull the features of a chimpanzee or the lineaments of a philosopher. These alleged restorations of ancient types of man have very little if any scientific value and are likely only to mislead the public... So put not your trust in reconstructions.[95]

Studies Made to Fabricate False Fossils

Unable to find valid evidence in the fossil record for the theory of evolution, some evolutionists have ventured to manufacture their own. These efforts, which have even been included in encyclopaedias under the heading "evolution forgeries", are the most telling indication that the theory of evolution is an ideology and a philosophy that evolutionists are hard put to defend. Two of the most egregious and notorious of these forgeries are described below.

Piltdown Man

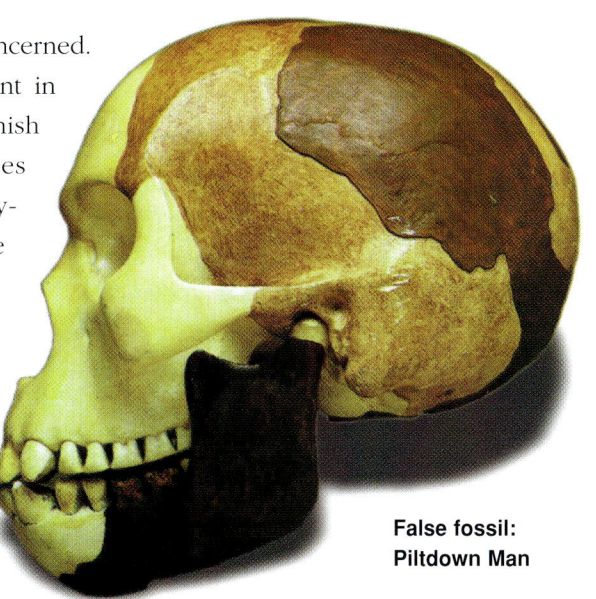

Charles Dawson, a well-known doctor and amateur paleoanthropologist, came forth with a claim that he had found a jawbone and a cranial fragment in a pit in the area of Piltdown, England, in 1912. Although the skull was human-like, the jawbone was distinctly simian. These specimens were christened the "Piltdown Man". Alleged to be 500 thousand years old, they were displayed as absolute proofs of human evolution. For more than 40 years, many scientific articles were written on the "Piltdown Man", many interpretations and drawings were made and the fossil was presented as crucial evidence of human evolution.

In 1949, scientists examined the fossil once more and concluded that the "fossil" was a deliberate forgery consisting of a human skull and the jawbone of an orang-utan.

Using the fluorine dating method, investigators discovered that the skull was only a few thousand years old. The teeth in the jawbone, which belonged to an orang-utan, had been artificially worn down and the "primitive" tools that had conveniently accompanied the fossils were crude forgeries that had been sharpened with steel implements. In the detailed analysis completed by Oakley, Weiner and Clark, they revealed this forgery to the public in 1953. The skull belonged to a 500-year-old man, and the mandibular bone belonged to a recently deceased ape! The teeth were thereafter specially arranged in an array and added to the jaw and the joints were filed in order to make them resemble that of a man. Then all these pieces were stained with potassium dichromate to give them a dated appearance. (These stains disappeared when dipped in acid.) Le Gros Clark, who was a member of the team that disclosed the forgery, could not hide his astonishment:

> The evidences of artificial abrasion immediately sprang to the eye. Indeed so obvious did they seem it may well be asked: how was it that they had escaped notice before?[96]

Nebraska Man

In 1922, Henry Fairfield Osborn, the director of the American Museum of Natural History, declared that he had found a molar tooth fossil in western Nebraska near Snake Brook belonging to the Pliocene period. This tooth allegedly bore the common characteristics of both man and ape. Deep scientific arguments began in which some interpreted this tooth to be that of Pithecanthropus erectus while others claimed it was closer to that of modern human beings. This fossil, which

The above picture was drawn based on a single tooth and it was published in the Illustrated London News of 24th July 1922. However, evolutionists were extremely disappointed when it was revealed that this tooth belonged neither to an ape-like creature nor to a man, but to an extinct species of pig.

aroused extensive debate, was popularly named "Nebraska Man". It was also immediately given a "scientific name": "Hesperopithecus Haroldcooki".

Many authorities gave Osborn their support. Based on this single tooth, reconstructions of Nebraska Man's head and body were drawn. Moreover, Nebraska Man was even pictured with a whole family.

In 1927, other parts of the skeleton were also found. According to these newly discovered pieces, the tooth belonged neither to a man nor to an ape. It was realised that it belonged to an extinct species of wild American pig called Prosthennops.

Did Men and Apes Come from a Common Ancestor?

According to the claims of the theory of evolution, men and modern apes have common ancestors. These creatures evolved in time and some of them became the apes of today, while another group that followed another branch of evolution became the men of today.

Evolutionists call the so-called first common ancestors of men and apes "Australopithecus" which means "South African ape". Australopithecus, nothing but an old ape species that has become extinct, has various types. Some of them are robust, while others are small and slight.

Evolutionists classify the next stage of human evolution as "Homo", that is "man". According to the evolutionist claim, the living beings in the Homo series are more developed than Australopithecus, and not very much different from modern man. The modern man of our day, Homo sapiens, is said to have formed at the latest stage of the evolution of this species.

The fact of the matter is that the beings called Australopithecus in this imaginary scenario fabricated by evolutionists really are apes that became extinct, and the beings in the Homo series are members of various human races that lived in the past and then disappeared. Evolutionists arranged various ape and human fossils in an order from the smallest to the biggest in order to form a "human evolution" scheme. Research, however, has demonstrated that these fossils by no means imply an evolutionary process and some of these alleged ancestors of man were real apes whereas some of them were real humans.

Now, let us have a look at Australopithecus, which represents to evolutionists the first stage of the scheme of human evolution.

Australopithecus: Extinct Apes

Evolutionists claim that Australopithecus are the most primitive ancestors of modern men. These are an old species with a head and skull structure similar to that of modern apes, yet with a smaller cranial capacity. According to the claims of evolutionists, these creatures have a very important feature that authenticates them as the ancestors of men: bipedalism.

The movements of apes and men are completely different. Human beings are the only living creatures that move freely about on two feet. Some other animals do have a limited ability to move in this way, but those that do have bent skeletons.

According to evolutionists, these living beings called Australopithecus had the ability to walk in a bent rather than an upright posture like human beings. Even this limited bipedal stride was sufficient to encourage evolutionists to project onto these creatures that they were the ancestors of man.

However, the first evidence refuting the allegations of evolutionists that Australopithecus were bipedal came from evolutionists themselves. Detailed studies made on Australopithecus fossils forced even evolutionists to admit that these looked "too" ape-like. Having conducted detailed anatomical research on Australopithecus fossils in the mid-1970s, Charles E. Oxnard likened the skeletal structure of Australopithecus to that of modern orang-utans:

> An important part of today's conventional wisdom about human evolution is based on studies of teeth, jaws and skull fragments of australopithecine fossils. These all indicate that the close relation of the australopithecine to the human lineage may not be true. All these fossils are different from gorillas, chimpanzees and men. Studied as a group, the australopithecine seems more like the orang-utan.[97]

What really embarrassed evolutionists was the discovery that Australopithecus could not have walked on two feet and with a bent posture. It would have been physically very ineffective for Australopithecus, allegedly bipedal but with a bent stride, to move about in such a way because of the enormous energy demands it would have entailed. By means of computer simulations conducted in 1996, the English paleoanthropologist Robin Crompton also demonstrated that such a "compound" stride was impossible. Crompton reached the following conclusion: a living being can walk either upright or on all fours. A type of in-between stride cannot be sustained for long periods because of the extreme energy consumption. This means that Australopithecus could not have been both bipedal and have a bent walking posture.

Probably the most important study demonstrating that Australopithecus could not have been bipedal came in 1994 from the research anatomist Fred Spoor and his team in the Department of Human Anatomy and Cellular Biology at the University of Liverpool, England. This group conducted studies on the bipedalism of fossilised living beings. Their research investigated the involuntary balance mechanism found in the cochlea of the ear, and the findings showed conclusively that Australopithecus could not have been bipedal. This precluded any claims that Australopithecus was human-like.

The Homo Series: Real Human Beings

The next step in the imaginary human evolution is "Homo", that is, the human series. These living beings are humans who are no different from modern men, yet who have some racial differences. Seeking to exaggerate these differences, evolutionists represent these people not as a "race" of modern man but as a different "species". However, as we will soon see, the people in the Homo series are nothing but ordinary human racial types.

According to the fanciful scheme of evolutionists, the internal imaginary evolution of the Homo species is as follows: First Homo erectus, then Homo sapiens archaic and Neanderthal Man, later Cro-Magnon Man and finally modern man.

Despite the claims of evolutionists to the contrary, all the "species" we have enumerated above are nothing but genuine human beings. Let us first examine Homo erectus, who evolutionists refer to as the most primitive human species.

The most striking evidence showing that Homo erectus is not a "primitive" species is the fossil of "Turkana Boy", one of the oldest Homo erectus remains. It is estimated that the fossil was of a 12-year-old boy, who would have been 1.83 meters tall in his adolescence. The upright skeletal structure of the fossil is no different from that of modern man. Its tall and slender skeletal structure totally complies with that of the people living in tropical regions in our day. This fossil is one of the most important pieces of evidence that Homo erectus is simply another specimen of the modern human race. Evolutionist paleontologist Richard Leakey compares Homo erectus and modern man as follows:

> One would also see differences in the shape of the skull, in the degree of protrusion of the face, the robustness of the brows and so on. These differences are probably no more pronounced than we see today between the separate geographical races of modern humans. Such biological variation arises when populations are geographically separated from each other for significant lengths of time.[98]

Leakey means to say that the difference between Homo erectus and us is no more than the difference between Negroes and Eskimos. The cranial features of Homo erectus resulted from their manner of feeding, and genetic emigration and from their not assimilating with other human races for a lengthy period.

Another strong piece of evidence that Homo erectus is not a "primitive" species is that fossils of this species have been unearthed aged twenty-seven thousand years and even thirteen thousand years. According to an article published in Time – which is not a scientific periodical, but nevertheless had a sweeping effect on the world of science – Homo erectus fossils aged twenty-seven thousand years were found on the island of Java. In the Kow swamp in Australia, some thirteen thousand year-old fossils were found that bore Homo Sapiens-Homo Erectus characteristics. All these fossils demonstrate that Homo erectus continued living up to times very close to our day and were nothing but a human race that has since been buried in history.

Archaic Homo Sapiens and Neanderthal Man

Archaic Homo sapiens is the immediate forerunner of contemporary man in the imaginary evolutionary scheme. In fact, evolutionists do not have much to say about these men, as there are only minor differences between them and modern men. Some researchers even state that representatives of this race are still living today, and point to the Aborigines in Australia as an example. Like Homo sapiens, the Aborigines also have thick protruding eyebrows, an inward-inclined mandibular structure, and a slightly smaller cranial volume. Moreover, significant discoveries have been made hinting that such people lived in Hungary and in some villages in Italy until not very long ago.

Evolutionists point to human fossils unearthed in the Neander valley of Holland which have been named Neanderthal Man. Many contemporary researchers define Neanderthal Man as a sub-species of modern man and call it "Homo sapiens neandertalensis". It is definite that this race lived together with modern humans, at the same time and in the same areas. The findings testify that Neanderthals buried their dead, fashioned musical instruments, and had cultural affinities with the Homo sapiens sapiens living during the same period. Entirely modern skulls and skeletal structures of Neanderthal fossils are not open to any speculation. A prominent authority on the subject, Erik Trinkaus from New Mexico University writes:

Detailed comparisons of Neanderthal skeletal remains with those of modern humans have shown that there is nothing in Neanderthal anatomy that conclusively indicates locomotor, manipulative, intellectual, or linguistic abilities inferior to those of modern humans.[99]

In fact, Neanderthals even had some "evolutionary" advantages over modern men. The cranial capacity of Neanderthals was larger than that of the modern man and they were more robust and muscular than we are. Trinkaus adds: "One of the most characteristic features of the Neanderthals is the exaggerated massiveness of their trunk and limb bones. All of the preserved bones suggest a strength seldom attained by modern humans. Furthermore, not only is this robustness present among the adult males, as one might expect, but it is also evident in the adult females, adolescents, and even children."

To put it precisely, Neanderthals are a particular human race that assimilated with other races in time.

All of these factors show that the scenario of "human evolution" fabricated by evolutionists is a figment of their imaginations, and that men have always been men and apes always apes.

Can Life Result from Coincidences as Evolution Argues?

The theory of evolution holds that life started with a cell that formed by chance under primitive earth conditions. Let us therefore examine the composition of the cell with simple comparisons in order to show how irrational it is to ascribe the existence of the cell – a structure which still maintains its mystery in many respects, even at a time when we are about to set foot in the 21st century – to natural phenomena and coincidences.

With all its operational systems, systems of communication, transportation and management, a cell is no less complex than any city. It contains power stations producing the energy consumed by the cell, factories manufacturing the enzymes and hormones essential for life, a databank where all necessary information about all products to be produced is recorded, complex transportation systems and pipelines for carrying raw materials and products from one place to another, advanced laboratories and refineries for breaking down imported raw materials into their usable parts, and specialised cell membrane proteins for the control of incoming and outgoing materials. These constitute only a small part of this incredibly complex system.

Far from being formed under primitive earth conditions, the cell, which in its composition and mechanisms is so complex, cannot be synthesised in even the most sophisticated laboratories of our day. Even with the use of amino acids, the building blocks of the cell, it is not possible to produce so much as a single organelle of the cell, such as mitochondria or ribosome, much less a whole cell. The first cell claimed to have been produced by evolutionary coincidence is as much a figment of the imagination and a product of fantasy as the unicorn.

Proteins Challenge Coincidence

And it is not just the cell that cannot be produced: the formation, under natural conditions, of even a single protein of the thousands of complex protein molecules making up a cell is impossible.

Proteins are giant molecules consisting of amino acids arranged in a particular sequence in certain quantities and structures. These molecules constitute the building blocks of a living cell. The simplest is composed of 50 amino acids; but there are some proteins that are composed of thousands of amino acids. The absence, addition, or replacement of a single amino acid in the structure of a protein in living cells, each of which has a particular function, causes the protein to become a useless molecular heap. Incapable of demonstrating the "accidental formation" of amino acids, the theory of evolution founders on the point of the formation of proteins.

We can easily demonstrate, with simple probability calculations anybody can understand, that the functional structure of proteins can by no means come about by chance.

There are twenty different amino acids. If we consider that an average-sized protein molecule is composed of 288 amino acids, there are 10^{300} different combinations of acids. Of all of these possible sequences, only "one" forms the desired protein molecule. The other amino-acid chains are either completely useless or else potentially harmful to living things. In other words, the probability of the coincidental formation of only one protein molecule cited above is "1 in 10^{300}". The probability of this "1" occurring out of an "astronomical" number consisting of 1 followed by 300 zeros is for all practical purposes zero; it is impossible. Furthermore, a protein molecule of 288 amino acids is rather a modest one compared with some giant protein molecules consisting of thousands of amino acids. When we apply similar probability calculations to these giant protein molecules, we see that even the word "impossible" becomes inadequate.

If the coincidental formation of even one of these proteins is impossible, it is billions of times more impossible for approximately one million of those proteins to come together by chance in an organised fashion and make up a complete human cell. Moreover, a cell is not merely a collection of proteins. In addition to proteins, cells also include nucleic acids, carbohydrates, lipids, vitamins, and many other chemicals such as electrolytes, all of which are arranged harmoniously and with design in specific proportions, both in terms of structure and function. Each functions as a building block or component in various organelles.

As we have seen, evolution is unable to explain the formation of even a single protein out of the millions in the cell, let alone explain the cell.

Prof. Dr. Ali Demirsoy, one of the foremost authorities of evolutionist thought in Turkey, in his book *Kalitim ve Evrim* (Inheritance and Evolution), discusses the probability of the accidental formation of Cytochrome-C, one of the essential enzymes for life:

> The probability of the formation of a Cytochrome-C sequence is as likely as zero. That is, if life requires a certain sequence, it can be said that this has a probability likely to be realised once in the whole universe. Otherwise, some metaphysical powers beyond our definition should have acted in its formation. To accept the latter is not appropriate to the goals of science. We therefore have to look into the first hypothesis.[100]

After these lines, Demirsoy admits that this probability, which he accepted just because it was "more appropriate to the goals of science", is unrealistic:

> The probability of providing the particular amino acid sequence of Cytochrome-C is as unlikely as the possibility of a monkey writing the history of humanity on a typewriter – taking it for granted that the monkey pushes the keys at random.[101]

The correct sequence of proper amino acids is simply not enough for the formation of one of the protein molecules present in living things. Besides this, each of the twenty different types of amino acid present in the composition of proteins must be left-handed. Chemically, there are two different types of amino acids called "left-handed" and "right-handed". The difference between them is the mirror-symmetry between their three dimensional structures, which is similar to that of a person's right and left hands. Amino acids of either of these two types are found in equal numbers in nature and they can bond perfectly well with one another. Yet, research uncovers an astonishing fact: all proteins present in the structure of living things are made up of left-handed amino acids. Even a single right-handed amino acid attached to the structure of a protein renders it useless.

Let us for an instant suppose that life came into existence by chance as evolutionists claim. In this case, the right and left-handed amino acids that were generated by chance should be present in nature in roughly equal amounts. The question of how proteins can pick out only left-handed amino acids, and how not even a single right-handed amino acid becomes involved in the life process is something that still confounds evolutionists. In the *Britannica Science Encyclopaedia*, an ardent defender of evolution, the authors indicate that the amino acids of all living organisms on earth and the building blocks of complex polymers such as proteins have the same left-handed asymmetry. They add that this is tantamount to tossing a coin a million times and always getting heads. In the same encyclopaedia, they state that it is not possible to understand why molecules become left-handed or right-handed and that this choice is fascinatingly related to the source of life on earth.[102]

It is not enough for amino acids to be arranged in the correct numbers, sequences, and in the required three-dimensional structures. The formation of a protein also requires that amino acid molecules with more than one arm be linked to each other only through certain arms. Such a bond is called a "peptide bond". Amino acids can make different bonds with each other; but proteins comprise those and only those amino acids that join together by "peptide" bonds.

Research has shown that only 50 % of amino acids, combining at random, combine with a peptide bond and that the rest combine with different bonds that are not present in proteins. To function properly, each amino acid making up a protein must join with other amino acids with a peptide bond, as it has only to be chosen from among the left-handed ones. Unquestionably, there is no control mechanism to select and leave out the right-handed amino acids and personally make sure that each amino acid makes a peptide bond with the other.

Under these circumstances, the probabilities of an average protein molecule comprising five hundred amino acids arranging itself in the correct quantities and in sequence, in addition to the probabilities of all of the amino acids it contains being only left-handed and combining using only peptide bonds are as follows:

– The probability of being in the right sequence
$= 1/20^{500} = 1/10^{650}$

– The probability of being left-handed
$= 1/2^{500} \quad\quad = 1/10^{150}$

– The probability of combining using a "peptide bond"
$= 1/2^{499} \quad\quad = 1/10^{150}$

TOTAL PROBABILITY
$= 1/10^{950}$ **that is, "1" probability in 10^{950}**

As you can see above, the probability of the formation of a protein molecule comprising five hundred amino acids is "1" divided by a number formed by placing 950 zeros after a 1, a number incomprehensible to the human mind. This is only a probability on paper. Practically, such a possibility has "0" chance of realisation. In mathematics, a probability smaller than 1 over 10^{50} is statistically considered to have a "0" probability of realisation.

While the improbability of the formation of a protein molecule made up of five hundred amino acids reaches such an extent, we can further proceed to push the limits of the mind to higher levels of improbability. In the "haemoglobin" molecule, a vital protein, there are five hundred and seventy-four amino acids, which is a much larger number than that of the amino acids making up the protein mentioned above. Now consider this: in only one out of the billions of red blood cells in your body, there are "280,000,000" (280 million) haemoglobin molecules. The supposed age of the earth is not sufficient to afford the formation of even a single protein, let alone a red blood cell, by the method of "trial and

> The probability of an average protein molecule comprising five hundred amino acids being arranged in the correct proportion and sequence in addition to the probability of all of the amino acids it contains being only left-handed and being combined only with peptide bonds is "1" divided by 10^{950}. We can write this number, which is formed by putting 950 zeros after 1, as follows:
>
> $$10^{950} =$$
>
> 100,000,000,000,000,000,000,000,000,000,000,000,000,000,000,000,000,
> 000,000,000,000,000,000,000,000,000,000,000,000,000,000,000,000,000,
> 000,000,000,000,000,000,000,000,000,000,000,000,000,000,000,000,000,
> 000,000,000,000,000,000,000,000,000,000,000,000,000,000,000,000,000,
> 000,000,000,000,000,000,000,000,000,000,000,000,000,000,000,000,000,
> 000,000,000,000,000,000,000,000,000,000,000,000,000,000,000,000,000,
> 000,000,000,000,000,000,000,000,000,000,000,000,000,000,000,000,000,
> 000,000,000,000,000,000,000,000,000,000,000,000,000,000,000,000,000,
> 000,000,000,000,000,000,000,000,000,000,000,000,000,000,000,000,000,
> 000,000,000,000,000,000,000,000,000,000,000,000,000,000,000,000,000,
> 000,000,000,000,000,000,000,000,000,000,000,000,000,000,000,000,000,
> 000,000,000,000,000,000,000,000,000,000,000,000,000,000,000,000,000,
> 000,000,000,000,000,000,000,000,000,000,000,000,000,000,000,000,000,
> 000,000,000,000,000,000,000,000,000,000,000,000,000,000,000,000,000,
> 000,000,000,000,000,000,000,000,000,000,000,000,000,000,000,000,000,
> 000,000,000,000,000,000,000,000,000,000,000,000,000

error". The conclusion from all this is that evolution falls into a terrible abyss of improbability right at the stage of the formation of a single protein.

Looking for Answers to the Generation of Life

Well aware of the terrible odds against the possibility of life forming by chance, evolutionists were unable to provide a rational explanation for their beliefs, so they set about looking for ways to demonstrate that the odds were not so unfavourable.

They designed a number of laboratory experiments to address the question of how life could generate itself from non-living matter. The best known and most respected of these experiments is the one known as the "Miller Experiment" or "Urey-Miller Experiment", which was conducted by the American researcher Stanley Miller in 1953.

With the purpose of proving that amino acids could have come into existence by accident, Miller created an atmosphere in his laboratory that he assumed would have existed on primordial earth (but which later proved to be unrealistic) and he set to work. The mixture he used for this primordial atmosphere was composed of ammonia, methane, hydrogen, and water vapour.

Miller knew that methane, ammonia, water vapour and hydrogen would not react with each other under natural conditions. He was aware that he had to inject energy into the mixture to start a reaction. He suggested that this energy could have come from lightning flashes in the primordial atmosphere and, relying on this supposition, he used an artificial electricity discharge in his experiments.

Miller boiled this gas mixture at 100 ºC for a week, and, in addition, he introduced an electric current into the chamber. At the end of the week, Miller analysed the chemicals that had been formed in the chamber and observed that three of the twenty amino acids, which constitute the basic elements of proteins, had been synthesised.

This experiment aroused great excitement among evolutionists and they promoted it as an outstanding success. Encouraged by the thought that this experiment definitely verified their theory, evolutionists immediately produced new scenarios. Miller had supposedly proved that amino acids could form by themselves. Relying on this, they hurriedly hypothesised the following stages. According to their scenario, amino acids had later by accident united in the proper sequences to form proteins. Some of these accidentally formed proteins placed themselves in cell membrane-like structures, which "somehow" came into existence and formed a primitive cell. The cells united in time and formed living organisms. The greatest mainstay of the scenario was Miller's experiment.

However, Miller's experiment was nothing but make-believe, and has since been proven invalid in many respects.

The Invalidity of Miller's Experiment

Nearly half a century has passed since Miller conducted his experiment. Although it has been shown to be invalid in many respects, evolutionists still advance Miller and his results as absolute proof that life could have formed spontaneously from non-living matter. When we assess Miller's experiment critically, without the bias and subjectivity of evolutionist thinking, however, it is evident that the situation is not as rosy as evolutionists would have us think. Miller set for himself the goal of proving that amino acids could form by themselves in earth's primitive conditions. Some amino acids were produced, but the conduct of the experiment conflicts with his goal in many ways, as we shall now see.

◆ Miller isolated the amino acids from the environment as soon as they were formed, by using a mechanism called a "cold trap". Had he not done so, the conditions of the environment in which the amino acids formed would immediately have destroyed the molecules.

It is quite meaningless to suppose that some conscious mechanism of this sort was integral to earth's primordial conditions, which involved ultraviolet radiation, thunderbolts, various chemicals, and a high percentage of free oxygen. Without such a mechanism, any amino acid that did manage to form would immediately have been destroyed.

◆ The primordial atmospheric environment that Miller attempted to simulate in his experiment was not realistic. Nitrogen and carbon dioxide would have been constituents of the primordial atmosphere, but Miller disregarded this and used methane and ammonia instead.

Why? Why were evolutionists insistent on the point that the primitive atmosphere contained high amounts of methane (CH_4), ammonia (NH_3), and water vapour (H_2O)? The answer is simple: without ammonia, it is impossible to synthesise an amino acid. Kevin McKean talks about this in an article published in Discover magazine:

> Miller and Urey imitated the ancient atmosphere of earth with a mixture of methane and ammonia. According to them, the earth was a true homogeneous mixture of metal, rock and ice. However in the latest studies, it is understood that the earth was very hot at those times and that it was composed of melted nickel and iron. Therefore, the chemical atmosphere of that time should have been formed mostly of nitrogen (N_2), carbon dioxide (CO_2) and water vapour (H_2O). However these are not as appropriate as methane and ammonia for the production of organic molecules.[103]

After a long period of silence, Miller himself also confessed that the atmospheric environment he used in his experiment was not realistic.

♦ Another important point invalidating Miller's experiment is that there was enough oxygen to destroy all the amino acids in the atmosphere at the time when evolutionists thought that amino acids formed. This oxygen concentration would definitely have hindered the formation of amino acids. This situation completely negates Miller's experiment, in which he totally neglected oxygen. If he had used oxygen in the experiment, methane would have decomposed into carbon dioxide and water, and ammonia would have decomposed into nitrogen and water.

On the other hand, since no ozone layer yet existed, no organic molecule could possibly have lived on earth because it was entirely unprotected against intense ultraviolet rays.

♦ In addition to a few amino acids essential for life, Miller's experiment also produced many organic acids with characteristics that are quite detrimental to the structures and functions of living things. If he had not isolated the amino acids and had left them in the same environment with these chemicals, their destruction or transformation into different compounds through chemical reactions would have been unavoidable. Moreover, a large number of right-handed amino acids also formed. The existence of these amino acids alone refuted the theory, even within its own reasoning, because right-handed amino acids are unable to function in the composition of living organisms and render proteins useless when they are involved in their composition.

To conclude, the circumstances in which amino acids formed in Miller's experiment were not suitable for life forms to come into being. The medium in which they formed was an acidic mixture that destroyed and oxidised any useful molecules that might have been obtained.

Evolutionists themselves actually refute the theory of evolution, as they are often wont to do, by advancing this experiment as "proof". If the experiment proves anything, it is that amino acids can only be produced in a controlled laboratory environment where all the necessary conditions have been specifically and consciously designed. That is, the experiment shows that what brings life (even the "near-life" of amino acids) into being cannot be unconscious chance, but rather conscious will – in a word, Creation. This is why every stage of Creation is a sign proving to us the existence and might of Allah.

The Miraculous Molecule: DNA

The theory of evolution has been unable to provide a coherent explanation for the existence of the molecules that are the basis of the cell. Furthermore, developments in the science of genetics and the discovery of the nucleic acids (DNA and RNA) have produced brand-new problems for the theory of evolution.

In 1955, the work of two scientists on DNA, James Watson and Francis Crick, launched a new era in biology. Many scientists directed their attention to the science of genetics. Today, after years of research, scientists have, largely, mapped the structure of DNA.

Here, we need to give some very basic information on the structure and function of DNA:

The molecule called DNA, which exists in the nucleus of each of the 100 trillion cells in our body, contains the complete construction plan of the human body. Information regarding all the characteristics of a person, from the physical appearance to the structure of the inner organs, is recorded in DNA by means of a special coding system. The information in DNA is coded within the sequence of four special bases that make up this molecule. These bases are specified as A, T, G, and C according to the initial letters of their names. All the structural differences among people depend on the variations in the sequence of these bases. There are approximately 3.5 billion nucleotides, that is, 3.5 billion letters in a DNA molecule.

The DNA data pertaining to a particular organ or protein is included in special components called "genes". For instance, information about the eye exists in a series of special genes, whereas information about the heart exists in quite another series of genes. The cell produces proteins by using the information in all of these genes. Amino acids that constitute the structure of the protein are defined by the sequential arrangement of three nucleotides in the DNA.

At this point, an important detail deserves attention. An error in the sequence of nucleotides making up a gene renders the gene completely useless. When we consider that there are 200 thousand genes in the human body, it becomes more evident how impossible it is for the mil-

The molecule called DNA contains the complete construction plan of the human body.

lions of nucleotides making up these genes to form by accident in the right sequence. An evolutionist biologist, Frank Salisbury, comments on this impossibility by saying:

> A medium protein might include about 300 amino acids. The DNA gene controlling this would have about 1,000 nucleotides in its chain. Since there are four kinds of nucleotides in a DNA chain, one consisting of 1,000 links could exist in 4^{1000} forms. Using a little algebra (logarithms), we can see that $4^{1000}=10^{600}$. Ten multiplied by itself 600 times gives the figure 1 followed by 600 zeros! This number is completely beyond our comprehension.[104]

The number 4^{1000} is equivalent to 10^{600}. We obtain this number by adding 600 zeros to 1. As 10 with 11 zeros indicates a trillion, a figure with 600 zeros is indeed a number that is difficult to grasp.

Evolutionist Prof. Ali Demirsoy was forced to make the following admission on this issue:

> In fact, the probability of the random formation of a protein and a nucleic acid (DNA-RNA) is inconceivably small. The chances against the emergence of even a particular protein chain are astronomic.[105]

In addition to all these improbabilities, DNA can barely be involved in a reaction because of its double-chained spiral shape. This also makes it impossible to think that it can be the basis of life.

Moreover, while DNA can replicate only with the help of some enzymes that are actually proteins, the synthesis of these enzymes can be realised only by the information coded in DNA. As they both depend on each other, either they have to exist at the same time for replication, or one of them has had to be "created" before the other. American microbiologist Jacobson comments on the subject:

> The complete directions for the reproduction of plans, for energy and the extraction of parts from the current environment, for the growth sequence, and for the effector mechanism translating instructions into growth – all had to be simultaneously present at that moment (when life began). This combination of events has seemed an incredibly unlikely happenstance, and has often been ascribed to divine intervention.[106]

The quotation above was written two years after the disclosure of the structure of DNA by James Watson and Francis Crick. Despite all the developments in science, this problem remains unsolved for evolutionists. To sum up, the need for DNA in reproduction, the necessity of the presence of some proteins for reproduction, and the requirement to produce these proteins according to the information in the DNA entirely demolish evolutionist theses.

Two German scientists, Junker and Scherer, explained that the synthesis of each of the molecules required for chemical evolution, necessitates distinct conditions, and that the probability of the compounding of these materials having theoretically very different acquirement methods is zero:

> Until now, no experiment is known in which we can obtain all the molecules necessary for chemical evolution. Therefore, it is essential to produce various molecules in different places under very suitable conditions and then to carry them to another place for reaction by protecting them from harmful elements like hydrolysis and photolysis.[107]

In short, the theory of evolution is unable to prove any of the evolutionary stages that allegedly occur at the molecular level.

To summarise what we have said so far, neither amino acids nor their products, the proteins making up the cells of living beings, could ever be produced in any so-called "primitive atmosphere" environment. Moreover, factors such as the incredibly complex structure of proteins, their right-hand, left-hand features, and the difficulties in the formation of peptide bonds are just parts of the reason why they will never be produced in any future experiment either.

Even if we suppose for a moment that proteins somehow did form accidentally, that would still have no meaning, for proteins are nothing at all on their own: they cannot themselves reproduce. Protein synthesis is only possible with the information coded in DNA and RNA molecules. Without DNA and RNA, it is impossible for a protein to reproduce. The specific sequence of the twenty different amino acids encoded in DNA determines the structure of each protein in the body. However, as has been made abundantly clear by all those who have studied these molecules, it is impossible for DNA and RNA to form by chance.

The Fact of Creation

With the collapse of the theory of evolution in every field, prominent names in the discipline of microbiology today admit the fact of creation and have begun to defend the view that everything is created by a conscious Creator as part of an exalted creation. This is already a fact that people cannot disregard. Scientists who can approach their work with an open mind have developed a view called "intelligent design". Michael J. Behe, one of the foremost of these scientists, states that he accepts the absolute being of the Creator and describes the impasse of those who deny this fact:

> The result of these cumulative efforts to investigate the cell – to investigate life at the molecular level – is a loud, clear, piercing cry of "design!" The result is so unambiguous and so significant that it must be ranked as one of the greatest achievements in the history of science. This triumph of science should evoke cries of "Eureka" from ten thousand throats.
>
> But, no bottles have been uncorked, no hands clapped. Instead, a curious, embarrassed silence surrounds the stark complexity of the cell. When the subject comes up in public, feet start to shuffle, and breathing gets a bit laboured. In private people are a bit more relaxed; many ex-

plicitly admit the obvious but then stare at the ground, shake their heads, and let it go like that. Why does the scientific community not greedily embrace its startling discovery? Why is the observation of design handled with intellectual gloves? The dilemma is that while one side of the elephant is labelled intelligent design, the other side must be labelled God.[108]

Today, many people are not even aware that they are in a position of accepting a body of fallacy as truth in the name of science, instead of believing in Allah. Those who do not find the sentence "Allah created you from nothing" scientific enough can believe that the first living being came into being by thunderbolts striking a "primordial soup" billions of years ago.

As we have described elsewhere in this book, the balances in nature are so delicate and so numerous that it is entirely irrational to claim that they developed "by chance". No matter how much those who cannot set themselves free from this irrationality may strive, the signs of Allah in the heavens and the earth are completely obvious and they are undeniable.

Allah is the Creator of the heavens, the earth and all that is in between.

The signs of His being have encompassed the entire universe.

Glory to You, of knowledge we have none, save what You have taught us: In truth it is You Who are perfect in knowledge and wisdom.
(Surat al-Baqara, 32)

NOTES

1 National Geographic, vol.165, no.6 , p. 775.
2 Bert Hölldobler-Edward O.Wilson, The Ants, Harvard University Press, 1990, p. 1.
3 Bilim ve Teknik Dergisi (Journal of Science and Technics), sayı: 190, s. 4.
4 Bert Hölldobler-Edward O.Wilson, The Ants, Harvard University Press, 1990, p. 330-331.
5 Focus Dergisi (Focus Magazine), October 1996.
6 Focus Dergisi (Focus Magazine), October 1996.
7 National Geographic, vol.165, no.6, p. 777.
8 Bert Hölldobler-Edward O.Wilson, The Ants, Harvard University Press, 1990, p. 227.
9 Ibid, p. 244.
10 Ibid, p. 2.
11 Ibid, p. 244.
12 Ibid, p. 197.
13 Ibid, p. 204.
14 Ibid, p. 293.
15 Ibid, p. 258.
16 Ibid, p. 255.
17 Ibid, p. 256.
18 Ibid, p. 257.
19 National Geographic, July 1995, p. 100.
20 Bert Hölldobler-Edward O.Wilson, The Ants, Harvard University Press, 1990, p. 597-598.
21 The Insects, Peter Farb and the Editors of Time-Life Books, p. 164.
22 National Geographic, July 1995, p. 104.
23 National Geographic, July 1995, p. 100.
24 National Geographic, July 1995, p. 104.
25 National Geographic, July 1995, p. 100.
26 National Geographic, July 1995, p. 104.
27 Harun Yahya, For Men of Understanding, Ta-Ha Publishers, 1999, p. 126-127
28 Bert Hölldobler-Edward O.Wilson, The Ants, Harvard University Press, 1990, p. 626.
29 The Insects, Peter Farb and the Editors of Time-Life Books, p. 163.
30 National Geographic, June 1984, p. 803.
31 Bilim ve Teknik Dergisi (Journal of Science and Technics), June 1978, no: 127, p.44.
32 National Geographic, June 1984, p. 813.
33 Bert Hölldobler-Edward O.Wilson, The Ants, Harvard University Press, 1990, p. 176-177, 450.
34 The Insects, Peter Farb and the Editors of Time-Life Books, p. 164.
35 Encyclopaedia of Animals, Maurice-Robert Burton, C.P.B.C Publishing Ltd., p. 14.
36 National Geographic, June 1984, p. 797.
37 National Geographic, June 1984, p. 801.
38 Encyclopaedia of Animals, Maurice-Robert Burton, C.P.B.C Publishing Ltd., p. 15.
39 Encyclopaedia of Animals, Maurice-Robert Burton, C.P.B.C Publishing Ltd., p. 199.
40 Encyclopaedia of Animals, Maurice-Robert Burton, C.P.B.C Publishing Ltd.
41 New Scientist, November 4, 1995, p. 29.
42 Bert Hölldobler-Edward O.Wilson, Journey to The Ants, Harvard University Press, Cambridge, 1994, p. 6.
43 Science, Vol.263, 18 March 1994.
44 Bert Hölldobler-Edward O.Wilson, The Ants, Harvard University Press, 1990, p. 512.
45 Ibid, p. 204.
46 Ibid.
47 Ibid, p. 486-487.
48 Ibid, p. 489.
49 Ecology, Michael Scott, Oxford University Press, New York, 1995, p. 33.
50 Bert Hölldobler-Edward O.Wilson, The Ants, Harvard University Press, 1990, p. 497-498.
51 Ibid, p. 500.
52 Ibid.
53 Ibid, p. 504.
54 Ibid, p. 507.
55 Ibid
56 Ibid, p. 506.
57 Ibid, p. 493.
58 Natural History, 1/94, Gregory Paulson and Roger D.Akre.
59 Bert Hölldobler-Edward O.Wilson, The Ants, Harvard University Press, 1990, p. 522-523.
60 Ibid, p. 530.

61 Ibid, p. 548.
62 Ibid, p. 531.
63 National Geographic Documentary
64 Bert Hölldobler-Edward O.Wilson, The Ants, Harvard University Press, 1990, p. 532
65 Ibid, p. 534-535
66 Geo Magazine, October 1995, p. 186
67 Bert Hölldobler-Edward O.Wilson, The Ants, Harvard University Press, 1990, p. 549
68 Natural History, 10/93, p. 4-8
69 Natural History, 10/93, p. 6
70 Bert Hölldobler-Edward O.Wilson, The Ants, Harvard University Press, 1990, p. 547
71 Ibid p. 535
72 Bert Hölldobler-Edward O.Wilson, Journey to The Ants, Harvard University Press, Cambridge, 1994, p. 70
73 Ibid, p. 71
74 Ibid, p. 67
75 Venomous Animals of the World, by Roger Caras, p. 84
76 Bert Hölldobler-Edward O.Wilson, The Ants, Harvard University Press, 1990, p. 284
77 Ibid, p. 185-186
78 National Geographic, June 1984, p. 790-791
79 Bert Hölldobler-Edward O.Wilson, Journey to The Ants, Harvard University Press, Cambridge, 1994, p. 30
80 Bert Hölldobler-Edward O.Wilson, The Ants, Harvard University Press, 1990, p. 374
81 Bert Hölldobler-Edward O.Wilson, Journey to The Ants, Harvard University Press, Cambridge, 1994, p. 195.
82 The Insects, by Peter Farb and the Editors of Time-Life Books, p. 170.
83 The Origin of Species, Charles Darwin, London: Senate Press, 1995, p. 273.
84 Bert Hölldobler-Edward O.Wilson, The Ants, Harvard University Press, 1990, p. 292
85 Ibid, p. 270-271.
86 Discover, January 1994, p. 63.
87 Bert Hölldobler-Edward O.Wilson, The Ants, Harvard University Press, 1990, p. 563
88 Science, Volume.262, 22 Oct 1993.
89 Bert Hölldobler-Edward O.Wilson, The Ants, Harvard University Press, 1990, p. 565
90. Charles Darwin, The Origin of Species: By Means of Natural Selection or the Preservation of Favoured Races in the Struggle for Life, London: Senate Press, 1995, p. 134.

91. Derek A. Ager. "The Nature of the Fossil Record." Proceedings of the British Geological Association, vol. 87, no. 2, (1976), p. 133.
92. T.N. George, "Fossils in Evolutionary Perspective", Science Progress, vol.48, (January 1960), p.1-3
93. Richard Monestarsky, Mysteries of the Orient, Discover, April 1993, p.40.
94. Stefan Bengston, Nature 345:765 (1990).
95. Earnest A. Hooton, Up From The Ape, New York: McMillan, 1931, p.332.
96. Stephen Jay Gould, Smith Woodward's Folly, New Scientist, 5 April, 1979, p. 44.
97. Charles E. Oxnard, The Place of Australopithecines in Human Evolution: Grounds for Doubt, Nature, No. 258, p. 389.
98. Richard Leakey, The Making of Mankind, London: Sphere Books, 1981, p. 116
99. Eric Trinkaus, Hard Times Among the Neanderthals, Natural History, No. 87, December 1978, p. 10, R.L. Holoway, "The Neanderthal Brain: What was Primitive?", American Journal of Physical Anthrophology Supplement, No. 12, 1991, p. 94
100. Ali Demirsoy, Kalitim ve Evrim (Inheritance and Evolution), Ankara: Meteksan Yayinlari 1984, p. 61
101. Ali Demirsoy, Kalitim ve Evrim (Inheritance and Evolution), Ankara: Meteksan Yayinlari 1984, p. 61
102. Fabbri Britannica Science Encyclopaedia, Vol. 2, No. 22, p. 519
103. Kevin McKean, Bilim ve Teknik, No. 189, p. 7
104. Frank B. Salisbury, "Doubts about the Modern Synthetic Theory of Evolution", American Biology Teacher, September 1971, p. 336.
105. Ali Demirsoy, Kalitim ve Evrim (Inheritance and Evolution), Ankara: Meteksan Publishing Co., 1984, p. 39.
106. Homer Jacobson, "Information, Reproduction and the Origin of Life", American Scientist, January, 1955, p.121.
107. Reinhard Junker & Siegfried Scherer, "Entstehung Gesiche Der Lebewesen", Weyel, 1986, p. 89.
108. Michael J. Behe, Darwin's Black Box, New York: Free Press, 1996, pp. 232-233.

ALSO BY HARUN YAHYA

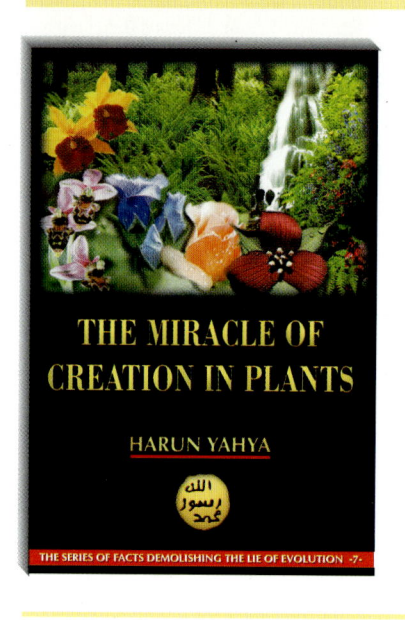

The purpose of this book is to display the miraculous features of plants and hence to make people see "the creation miracle" in things -they often encounter in the flow of their daily lives and sidestep.

This book opens new horizons on these issues for people who, throughout their lives, - think only about their own needs and hence fail to see the evidence of Allah's existence. Reading and understanding this book will be an important step in coming to an understanding of one's Creator.

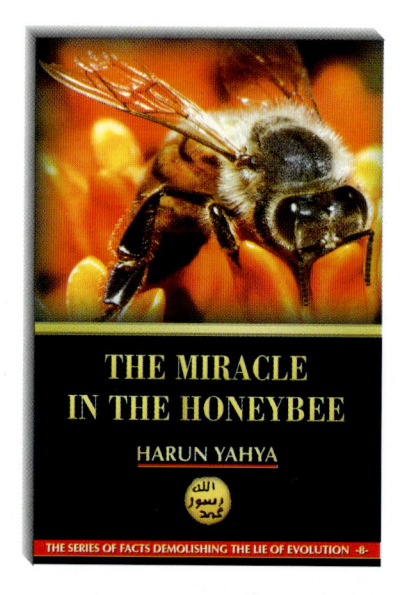

200 PAGES WITH 179 PICTURES IN COLOUR

In the Qur'an, Allah draws our attention to a number of creatures and summons man to ponder them. The honeybee is one of these. In Surat an-Nahl, "The surah of the honeybee", we are told that this creature's behaviour is inspired by Allah to produce honey, a benefit for man.

A thorough examination of the honeybee reveals its miraculous features. Research on honeybees indicates that these living beings employ a remarkable system of communication among themselves while the honeycombs they build are based on precise calculations that human beings could not duplicate without proper tools. Details concerning the life of honeybees furnish evidence for the creation of Allah.

200 PAGES WITH 179 PICTURES IN COLOUR

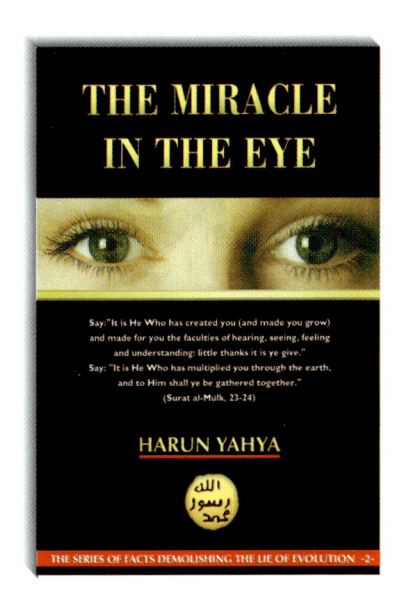

This book reveals the "miracle in the eye" In it, you will find a description of a perfect system and the story of the unbelievable events taking place behind the hundreds of eyes we see each day... As in all the books of this series, this one discusses the theory of evolution in detail and the collapse of that theory is proven once more. When you read the book, you will see how right Darwin was when he said "The thought of the eye makes me cold all over."

123 PAGES WITH 76 PICTURES IN COLOUR

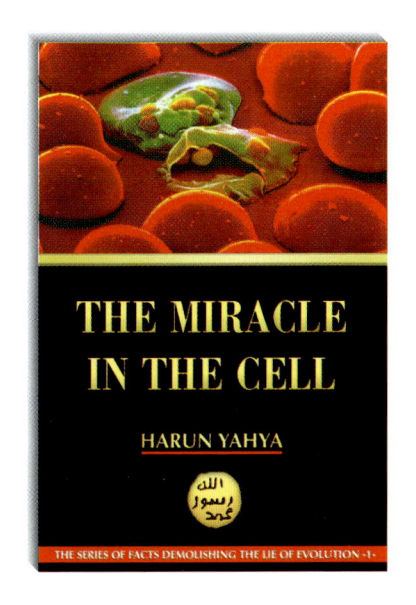

147 PAGES WITH 82 PICTURES IN COLOUR

The cell is one of the main subjects taught in biology classes, but most of the time, what is taught in these classes is quickly forgotten after school. The reason is that in school, the subject of the cell is presented in a very misleading manner. The method employed is based exclusively on a bald description of the extraordinarily complex organelles and the amazing processes going on in the cell. All that is related is the "what" of the cell; never is there any mention of "how" this extraordinary biological machine could have come into being.

This is because the "scientists" who have developed this deceptive method know full well that there is no answer to the question that is sure to follow "Then who created the cell?" other than acknowledging the existence of a Creator. This book deals primarily with the answer to that question.

THE MIRACLE IN THE SPIDER

HARUN YAHYA

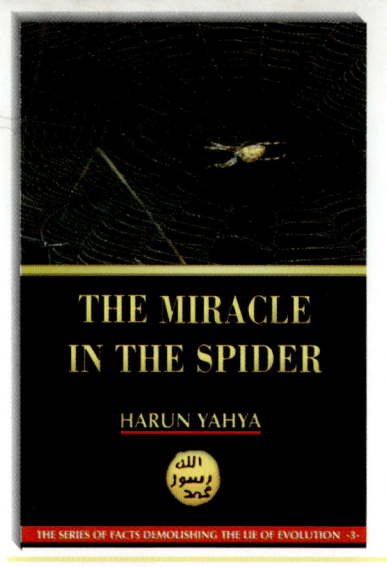

This is not a biological treatise on the tiny creature called a spider. It is indeed about the spider but the reality it reveals and the message it gives is much more significant. Just as a tiny key opens a huge door, this book will open new horizons for its readers. And the reality behind that door is the most important reality that one can come across in one's lifetime. Relating the amazing and admirable features of spiders known by few people and asking the questions of "how" and "why" in the process, this book reveals the excellence and perfection inherent in Allah's creation.

92 PAGES WITH 102 PICTURES IN COLOUR

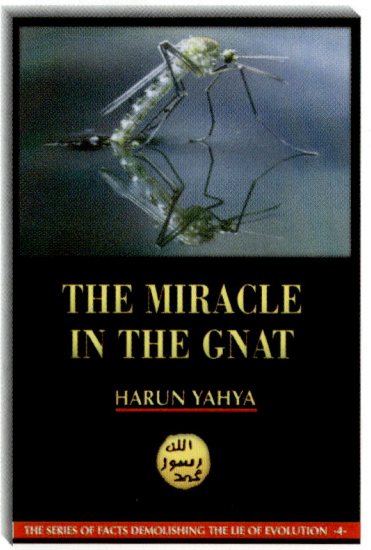

THE MIRACLE IN THE GNAT

HARUN YAHYA

In the Qur'an it is stated **"Surely Allah is not ashamed to set forth any parable- (that of) a gnat or any thing above that..."** (Surat al-Baqara: 26), because even so tiny a creature is full of the signs of Allah's excellent creation. By examining this tiny animal, one comes to realize that life could not have originated by itself but had to have been created by a Creator, who is Allah, Possessor of eternal wisdom and knowledge and able to do all things.
This book is written to help clarify this concept by drawing attention to the amazing features of the gnat.

62 PAGES WITH 41 PICTURES IN COLOUR

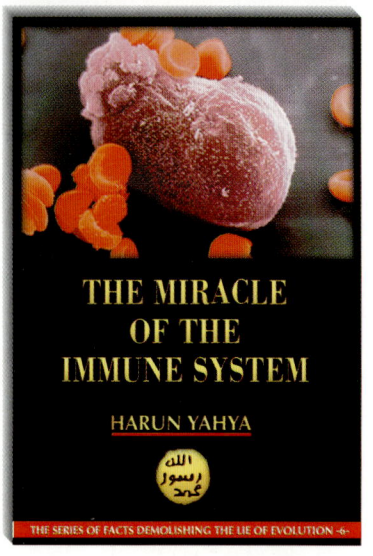

THE MIRACLE OF THE IMMUNE SYSTEM

HARUN YAHYA

We fall sick many times throughout our lives. When the events of "sickness" and "recovering" take place, our bodies become a battleground in which a bitter struggle is taking place. Microbes invisible to our eyes intrude into our body and begin to increase rapidly. The body however has a mechanism that combats them. Known as the "immune system", this mechanism is the most disciplined, most complex and successful army of the world. This system proves that the human body is the outcome of a unique design that has been planned with a great wisdom and skill. In other words, the human body is the evidence of a flawless creation, which is the peerless creation of Allah.

152 PAGES WITH 125 PICTURES IN COLOUR